In Whose Image?

In Whose Image?
Faith, Science, and the New Genetics

John P. Burgess, Editor

Published for the
Office of Theology and Worship
Congregational Ministries Division
Presbyterian Church (U.S.A.)
by

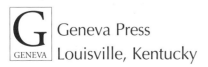

Geneva Press
Louisville, Kentucky

© The Office of Theology and Worship,
Congregational Ministries Division, Presbyterian Church (U.S.A.)

Scripture quotations from the New Revised Standard Version
of the Bible are copyright © 1989 by the Division of Christian Education
of the National Council of the Churches of Christ in the U.S.A. and are used
by permission.

Book design by Carol Eberhart Johnson
Cover design by Kevin Darst

First edition
Published by Geneva Press
Louisville, Kentucky

This book is printed on acid-free paper that meets the
American National Standards Institute Z39.48 standard. ∞

PRINTED IN THE UNITED STATES OF AMERICA
98 99 00 01 02 03 04 05 06 07 — 10 9 8 7 6 5 4 3 2 1

Library of Congress Cataloging-in-Publication Data

In whose image? : faith, science, and the new genetics / John P.
Burgess, editor.
    p.   cm.
Includes bibliographical references.
ISBN 0-664-50025-0 (alk. paper)
    1. Religion and science.   2. Man (Christian theology)
3. Presbyterian Church (U.S.A.)—Doctrines.   I. Burgess, John P.,
1954–   .
BL240.2.I475   1998
261.5′5—DC21   98-11934

Contents

Preface

The 202nd General Assembly (1990) of the Presbyterian Church (U.S.A.) approved an overture from the Presbytery of National Capital, asking the church to "develop, produce, and distribute study materials . . . concerning the theological and ethical issues raised by the Human Genome Project, in particular, and genetic research and development, in general." The overture noted that the results of genetic research challenge traditional theological understandings of the creation of humanity as being "in the image of God." The overture also referred to questions of the omnipotence of God, of the role of God in determining the future of humanity, and of the relationship between God and humanity.

Four years later, the 206th General Assembly (1994) approved an overture from the Presbytery of Pittsburgh, asking the church to "engage in an inquiry into the theological and ethical significance of contemporary physical, biological, and human sciences for the Reformed doctrines of humanity and sin." The overture called on the church to reformulate the church's understanding of humanity and sin in light of contemporary scientific findings.

The denomination's Office of Theology and Worship (in the Christian Faith and Life Area of the Congregational Ministries Division), in consultation and cooperation with the Advisory Committee on Social

Witness Policy, has coordinated work on these overtures. This volume of essays represents the first fruits of this labor, a significant effort by one mainline denomination to reflect on the Christian faith in light of changes in science and technology.

In planning the volume, the Office of Theology and Worship and the Advisory Committee on Social Witness Policy constituted a work group representing a diverse group of scientists, theologians, pastors, and lay people. Particular thanks are due to each of its members: Lowanna Askew, James Ayers, I. Lehr Brisbin, R. David Cole, Ronald Cole-Turner, James C. Goodloe IV, Samuel Gregorio, Stephen Hsieh, Gerald McKenny, James B. Miller, R. Scott Poethig, and Margaret Gray Towne. Several members of the work group drafted chapters; every member was involved in reading and commenting on them. In addition, Susan L. Nelson graciously agreed to contribute a chapter.

Thanks are also due to several other persons. At various times, Lynne Ballerstedt, John P. Burgess, and Joseph D. Small III from the Office of Theology and Worship, and Peter Sulyok from the Advisory Committee on Social Witness Policy, provided staff support to the work group. Dora G. Lodwick and Gaspar B. Langella, on behalf of the Advisory Committee on Social Witness Policy, reviewed and commented on earlier drafts of the chapters. C. Ray Trout of the Presbyterian Publishing Corporation provided valuable assistance in guiding the project to publication.

In the end, the work group was concerned not to produce a consensus statement or a policy document, but to provide a basic introduction to the kinds of issues that face the church.

While the essays ask the reader to learn some basic biological and theological vocabulary, they seek to speak to a broad church audience, not just to experts in these fields. Members of the work group hope that their commitment to thoughtful conversation might serve as a model to the church as others now read, and respond to, the essays.

How to Use This Book

This volume lends itself well to both personal and group study. The introductory essay provides an overview of each chapter, as well as a discussion of the basic themes that run through the volume as a whole. In addition, a summary and study questions appear at the end of each essay. Questions for further reflection on the volume as a whole are listed at its end.

Two ways for study leaders to proceed are suggested below:

Study Plan A

1. Proceed through the book in the order in which the chapters appear, beginning with the introductory essay. Such a class would need at least nine sessions (that is, a session to introduce participants to the book, then one session for each of the eight chapters).
2. Have people read a chapter ahead of each class meeting. They may wish to answer the questions at the end of the chapter on their own. If possible, designate one person to present a five-to-ten-minute overview of the chapter at the next session.
3. Open each class meeting with prayer.
4. If a person was designated, have that person give a five-to-ten-minute overview of the chapter.
5. Ask people for their reactions to the chapter. What intrigued them or disturbed them? What did they not understand? (It may be helpful to have a scientist available as a resource person throughout the class. Such a person might be recruited from a local high

school or college, if no one in the congregation is available.)
6. Read aloud the summary that appears at the end of the chapter. Then, discuss the study questions for that chapter.
7. Ask people what difference, if any, the ideas in this chapter make for the way we live our lives as Christians. How can our new knowledge teach us to be more faithful to God? What do we need to learn from scripture and our theological tradition in order to respond to these developments in the sciences? If you wish, refer to the questions for further reflection at the end of the volume.

Study Plan B

1. Rather than reading the entire book, focus on two or three chapters. Study the chapters in Part I, Part II, or Part III, or mix chapters from different parts of the book. Such a class would need four or five sessions (one for each chapter, plus one introductory meeting and one concluding meeting—see below).
2. After opening with prayer, divide the first meeting into two parts. For the first half of the meeting, give an overview of the material in the introductory essay. For the second half of the meeting, give an overview of the chapter that group members will be reading for the coming week. (During the week, group members may wish to answer the questions at the end of the chapter on their own.)
3. Divide each of the next meetings into two parts, again opening each with prayer. For the first half of the meeting, ask people for their reactions to the chapter. What intrigued them or disturbed them? What did they not understand? What are the central issues that need to be discussed?
4. For the second half of the meeting, give an overview of the material for next week. During this overview, you might also read aloud the summary and/or the study questions for the chapter that the group will be discussing.
5. At the last meeting, ask people what difference, if any, the ideas in this course make for the way we live our lives as Christians. How can our new knowledge teach us to be more faithful to God? What do we need to learn from scripture and our theological tradition in order to respond to these developments in the sciences? If you wish, refer to the questions for further reflection at the end of the volume.

An Introductory Essay: Searching for Meaning in a Brave, New World

John P. Burgess

This volume of essays reflects a growing interest in the church in the relationship between religion and science. The particular focus of the volume is the challenge that contemporary developments in the biological sciences pose to the church's theology and, especially, to the church's understanding of what it means to be human before God.

The authors of these essays represent the Reformed tradition. Their questions, however, speak to all Christians. Can Christians affirm both their own faith and the findings of contemporary science? Where do Christians need to rethink traditional doctrines in light of these findings? Where does the Christian tradition contain insights that might help us to assess the potential good, as well as evil, of contemporary developments in genetic research?

While some of these questions are of particular interest to Christians who happen to be scientists, they increasingly concern us all. As we learn of scientific breakthroughs, we enjoy the possibilities of new technologies but also face immensely complex decisions about such matters as who lives and who dies, the relationship between economic progress and environmental protection, and the ends of a good life and a good society. Contemporary developments in the sciences challenge each of us as members of the church to take stock of the responsible exercise of human power, so that we might seek just and wise solutions, faithful to the will of God.

Overview

Part I (chapters 1–3) sets the context. Each chapter argues that the church has nothing to fear from opening itself to the findings of contemporary science. While these findings challenge the church to rethink its theology, they do not require the church to abandon it.

In chapter 1, Margaret Towne asks the church to engage in a process of critical thinking. Rather than simply adhering to inherited positions, the church is called to a posture of "informed skepticism." Scientific findings need not threaten the church, if we are able to see them as opening us more fully to God and God's work. Critical thinking can stir us to a sense of wonder at all that God is doing.

In chapter 2, James Miller offers a brief historical overview of relations between science and religion. Three major periods, each with a distinctive worldview, emerge. The Classical period, up to the time of the Enlightenment, saw reality as an organic whole. The Modern period, beginning with the Enlightenment, saw reality in mechanistic and dualistic terms, with spirit separate from matter, mind from body, and (inevitably) religion from science. The Emergent (or "Postmodern") period, our own, teaches us to see reality in terms of history, development, and change. Again, the church is challenged to rethink its theology in light of the time in which it finds itself.

In chapter 3, James Ayers looks at a biblical text, Genesis 1, that has often lain at the heart of debates about Christianity and the theory of evolution. Some Christians have seen Genesis 1 as providing scientific evidence for God's activity of creating the world; some scientists (and Christians), by contrast, have dismissed it as a fanciful myth. Ayers argues that Genesis 1 is best understood as a hymn of praise. It does not lie in opposition to contemporary understandings of nature. Rather, it testifies to the reality of God, whose mysterious yet gracious ways are apparent in the processes of nature.

Part II (chapters 4–5) offers an overview of the biological sciences and their implications for our understanding of humanity. These chapters argue against simplistic notions of biological determinism. While biological factors profoundly influence human behavior, they interact in complex ways with other factors, including human freedom.

In chapter 4, David Cole describes the processes by which genes guide human development (an understanding of which also assists us in understanding recent experimentation with the cloning of animals). While genes set the potentials and limitations of human beings, one or two genes cannot account by themselves for how a person will actually behave in a particular situation. First, most human characteristics and behaviors are the result of complex interactions among many genes, not just one or two. Second, environmental factors—both physical and social—regulate which genes will express themselves in particular situations. Third, personal choices can moderate or modify genetic influences.

In chapter 5, I. Lehr Brisbin discusses human evolution and the place of human beings in the biological world. On the one hand, humans from a genetic point of view are not as different from other animals, especially the great apes, as much of Christian theology once asserted. Nor are genetic differences among humans as great as differences in appearance and culture might suggest. On the other hand, these genetic differences are greater than would have occurred without language differences that have isolated groups from each other. This genetic diversity—real, though limited—is part of the rich inheritance of the human species.

Part III (chapters 6–8) offers theological reflections on what it means to be human. These chapters explore such notions as the image of God, the spirit, the soul, free will, and sin. While none of these chapters offers a fully-developed proposal for a contemporary doctrine of humanity, together they do suggest the kinds of questions that theologians—and the church—must consider in response to the findings of the biological sciences.

In chapter 6, Susan Nelson looks at the human condition from a biblical theological perspective. While acknowledging a diversity of perspectives within scripture, Nelson, informed in part by feminist readings of scripture, delineates key theological themes and tensions that run throughout the Bible.

In chapter 7, James Goodloe examines questions of humanity and sin from the perspective of Reformed confessions. Goodloe draws out insights that may assist Christians in making sense of both the validity and limitations of contemporary scientific claims (and of popular conceptions about these claims).

In chapter 8, Ronald Cole-Turner reflects more explicitly on the implications of contemporary genetic research for theology, as well as on the kinds of questions that the church might pose as society determines how to use the new powers that genetic research provides. Insights from Christian scripture and theology again frame key themes and tensions.

Theological Issues

While this volume does not provide a systematic treatment of the complex questions that contemporary developments in genetic research pose, these essays might help to stimulate the church's discussion in several areas:

1. *The Image of God.* All these essays seek to deepen our understanding of what makes humans "human." From a Christian perspective, however, the question of humanity cannot be separated from the question of God. As Goodloe notes, Reformed confessions implicitly tell us who we are by reminding us of who God is—and of how we are not God (not infinite, not almighty, etc.), yet are related to God.

It is therefore appropriate that several of these essays discuss what it means to be created "in the image of God," a matter that Christian theology has long debated. As Nelson points out, Christian theologians have at one time or another appealed to human capacities of reasoning, of dominating other creatures, and of transcending some of the limitations of nature and history as evidence that humans are uniquely created in the image of God.

These essays take a different tack. Rather than equating creation in the image of God with one set of human capacities or another, they suggest a basic tension in the human condition. On the one hand, Brisbin, Nelson, and Cole-Turner argue that humans are not as different from other animals as we might like to believe. As Brisbin notes, scientists have found that some of the characteristics traditionally assigned to humans alone, such as an awareness of death, are not absent from the animal world. The relationship between humans and other animals is best understood as a continuum, not an opposition.

On the other hand, humans are unlike other animals in important respects. Nelson, Goodloe, and Cole-Turner argue that humans are uniquely related to the divine. We have a sense of "something more" (Nelson). We are created to worship God (Goodloe). We are spiritual and moral agents (Cole-Turner). Indeed, as Christians we claim a history of relationship to God, to which scripture witnesses: from God's choosing of a people in Abraham to God's choosing of a new people in the death and resurrection of Jesus Christ.

As Nelson says, we are made in the image of God, yet we are not as central to God's creation as we might like. Human salvation is not God's only end. God takes delight in the whole creation.

2. *The Soul.* This tension—that we are "just" animals, yet more than "just" animals—complicates the way we think about the soul. Goodloe argues that the Reformed tradition has seen the soul as the self. As souls, we are free, responsible, and self-conscious persons. Goodloe notes that this position leads to a dualism of soul and body, with the soul somehow more essential to human identity than the body. While acknowledging that this dualism may be too strong, especially in light of contemporary understandings of humanity, Goodloe believes that the Reformed confessions guard against the opposite extreme: a reduction of humans to physical functions or chemical reactions.

Nelson and Cole-Turner reject this dualism more vigorously. Nelson reminds us that we do not simply "have" bodies; rather, we "are" bodies. The soul is best understood not in opposition to the body, but as the enlivened body. In addition, argues Nelson, humans are spirit. They are free. They can choose God or reject God.

Cole-Turner defines the soul as humans' unique capacities for language, moral awareness, free choice, creativity, and relationship with God. Our genes in interaction with our environment help to define these capacities. There is no abstract self, no soul that exists apart from the body.

While these different ways of defining soul may confuse us, they suggest the complexity of the questions that we face. For Goodloe, it is soul more than body that makes us "human." For Nelson and Cole-Turner, by contrast, our bodies are essential to our human nature, yet our bodies do not simply determine us but also provide for the possibility of our freedom. Nelson locates this capacity for freedom in "spirit"; Cole-Turner calls it "soul." Despite these differences in terminology, all three essays reflect on the word "soul" in order to get at a basic tension in the human condition: free will versus determinism.

3. *Free Will versus Determinism.* Christian theology has long debated the question of the freedom of the human will. On the one hand, traditional Christian theology in the West has argued that the human will is bound. Ever since Adam and Eve disobeyed God, humans have no longer been able to choose the good that God intends for them. The human decision to sin is inevitable. On the other hand, traditional Christian theology has argued that humans are responsible for their sin, even if their sin is inevitable. We are somehow both free and determined.

A similar tension has characterized the question of redemption. Traditional Christian theology, especially as reformulated at the time of the Reformation, has insisted that salvation comes by God's grace alone. No human effort merits God's grace; every human effort to do the good is flawed and distorted. Yet God's grace, rather than eliminating human free will, restores it. God's grace frees us; it does not manipulate us. Again, we are somehow both free and determined.

As Cole-Turner points out, the findings of genetic research raise the question of free will versus determinism (or, to use Nelson's term, dependency) in yet another form. To the popular mind, contemporary science seems to argue that our genes determine our behaviors. When we hear that specific genes account for alcoholism, depression, or other disorders, we may be tempted to conclude that genes also account for our choice of good or evil.

These essays suggest that the picture is more complicated. Cole and Cole-Turner argue that human behaviors result from a complex interplay of genetic, environmental, and personal/historical factors, including our choices. Genes may predispose us to act in certain ways, but they never simply determine us. As Cole demonstrates, just as environmental factors force our bodies to adapt, so too certain behaviors (such as learning) influence which of our genes will come to expression. Cole calls for a "creative synergy" (that is, creative expression of our freedom within the constraints of genes and environment) in which we would seek to maximize the good that our genes allow us.

4. *Beyond Dualism?* While Cole retains the term "free will," he

argues that genes and environment severely constrain human freedom. Cole-Turner further develops this line of thought. To him, once we acknowledge that the human will is limited by genetic and environmental factors, we can no longer understand human freedom as absolute or disembodied. He therefore seeks a new language for talking about the human condition, so as to avoid the dualism that the language of free will and determinism may suggest. The paradoxes of the human condition, such as "determined, yet free," give way to a view of the human as a constantly evolving system of possibilities and limitations, a "feedback system" (see Cole), a "history" (see Miller).

The evolutionary picture that Brisbin describes further reinforces this picture of humans as a set of complex interactions in which genes, environment, and human choices and history all play a role. Cole-Turner emphasizes that these interactions shape *individuals* in profoundly different ways; Brisbin notes that these interactions have also contributed to genetic diversity among different *groups* within the human family.

Just as Cole-Turner asks us to move beyond dualism in characterizing the human condition, Brisbin challenges us to move beyond friend-enemy thinking in human relationships. From an evolutionary point of view, there is more that unites humans than divides us. The fact of genetic diversity, reflecting a rich history of human adaptation, need not be an obstacle to human relationships; on the contrary, an appreciation of this diversity can testify more fully to what it means to be created in the image of God.

5. *Implications for Our Life before God.* Cole-Turner argues that this complex interplay of genetic, environmental, and personal/historical factors accounts as much for our relationship with God as for other areas of human life and behavior. We do not lead a "spiritual life" that is somehow disconnected from the rest of us.

Cole-Turner raises the possibility that we could someday seek to alter our genetic code for the sake of deepening certain states of spiritual consciousness. While he refuses to reject such alterations out of hand, he notes the ambivalence that he and most of us feel about such alterations. We might ask ourselves, "At what point are we no longer simply cooperating with God but seeking to become God?"

Goodloe's essay helps to suggest more fully the character of this ambivalence. Drawing on Reformed theology, Goodloe reminds us that in this life we can never fully transcend the limitations of created beings. First, God has created us as finite (limited, ultimately, by death). While we properly take action to ameliorate human suffering and limitation, we can never escape them entirely. We are finally in God's hands.

Second, we can never escape sin entirely. The best of our efforts are flawed, self-interested, and pretentious. We easily forget God and worship the work of our own minds and hands. While we should seek the good that genetic alterations may offer, we should never fool ourselves into believing that we are therefore less dependent on God's mercy and grace. (On this point, also see Nelson.)

6. *Science and Religion.* These issues finally return us to the question of the proper relationship between science and religion. Each of these essays affirms that science and religion should be in dialogue. Each affirms that the church should be open to the truth that science seeks. Each affirms that science is a human enterprise, subject to correction.

Beyond these points of agreement, differences of emphasis remain. One emphasis, represented particularly well by Miller, wants to move us beyond a dualism of science and religion. The church must open itself to science more fully than it has in the past. It need not accept the results of science uncritically, but it dare not ignore them.

To use Miller's analogy, science and religion can blend their voices into a rich harmony. They can enrich each other. Moreover, to move beyond dualism may suggest that the church must avoid a dualism that places God on one side and humanity on the other; after all, God has entered the world, ultimately in the life of Jesus.

A second emphasis, represented particularly well by Ayers, wants to move us to worship. The point is less how to bring science and religion into harmony than how to see the world, through the eyes of scripture, as God's marvelous creation. Understood properly and kept within its proper limits, science can contribute to a deeper sense of wonder at God and God's ways.

A third emphasis, represented particularly well by Towne, wants to move us to think critically. Science and religion may harmonize.

They may evoke wonder. But they also question each other. They have the capacity to keep each other honest, so that we are better able to acknowledge both the possibilities and limitations of their claims to truth.

What's Missing?

This volume is limited in scope. A more complete explication of the current issues would necessarily include the following:

1. The theological and ethical implications of germ-line interventions (that is, alterations of one's genetic code that can be passed from one generation to the next).
2. The theological and ethical implications of (human) cloning.
3. Whether we can speak meaningfully of "normalcy," if genetic mutation and diversity are basic biological realities.
4. Theological developments since the Reformation, including contemporary critical theologies, that could assist us in responding to the challenges posed by developments in the sciences.
5. How an understanding of genetic diversity might illuminate or obscure racial differences (for example, the question of the role that genes do or do not play in cognitive ability).
6. The contributions of studies in the history and sociology of science, which make us aware of the social conditions under which scientific discoveries occur and can be (mis)used to safeguard the power of particular social groups.
7. The implications of genetic research and genetic engineering for a whole array of ethical issues (including questions of the appropriate use of technologies in altering the human genome, and questions of the appropriate use of information about individuals' genetic codes).

The authors hope that these essays, despite their limitations, will encourage the wider church to reflect on these issues. Only if the church is versed in the state of genetic research and has reflected on its basic theological and ethical implications will it be able to offer guidance on these matters to its members and the wider society.

PART I

INTERACTIONS BETWEEN SCIENCE
AND RELIGION

Chapter 1

Great and Hidden Things: Science, Religion, and Critical Thinking

Margaret Gray Towne

The Wonder, and Challenge, of New Knowledge

Thus says the LORD who made the earth, the LORD who formed it to establish it—the LORD is his name: Call to me and I will answer you, and will tell you great and hidden things that you have not known. (Jeremiah 33:2–3)

What an astounding declaration to hear from God, Creator of the universe! Would we ever be so fortunate to receive such a promise? The answer is, "Yes!" Great and hidden things are constantly being revealed by the God who said, "I am about to do a new thing" (Isaiah 43:19).

This God gave us the Ten Commandments and then a new commandment, to "love one another" (John 13:34). This God asked annually for a sacrificed lamb to atone for sin, yet in the fullness of time provided the universal sacrificial Lamb, once for all. In Jesus Christ, this God walked among us, talked like us, looked like us, worked like us, ate, slept, prayed, cried, died, was buried . . . and then rose from the grave! There is no doubt: this God does new things!

In recent centuries, many people might have identified with astronomer and mathematician Johannes Kepler (1571–1630), who exclaimed at the end of his work on planetary motion, "I give thanks to

Thee, O Lord Creator, Who hast delighted me with Thy makings, and in the works of Thy hands have I exulted."[1] New and hidden things in God's vast universe are there for the finding if we have curiosity, openness to new ideas, the capability to learn, and determination.

These discoveries regularly inspire awe and worship among those who acknowledge God as Creator. "Before these mysteries of life," exclaimed Jean Henri Fabre, the entomologist, after he had studied the process of cross-pollination of flowers by insects, "reason bows and abandons itself to adoration of the Author of these miracles."[2]

Through Kepler, Pasteur, Einstein, Newton, Galileo, Mendel, Darwin, Lyell, Wegener, Curie, and innumerable others, God has introduced us to great and wondrous surprises. "That this is God's world and that he is at work in it, creating, sustaining, redeeming—this we must receive as the indispensable 'given' for a meaningful approach to reality."[3] "God is no mere archivist unfolding an infinite sequence he had designed once and forever. He continues the labor of creation throughout time."[4]

Our lives have been powerfully affected by the explosion of new knowledge in science, and by subsequent technology (application of that knowledge). Computers, jets, anesthesia, internal combustion engines, VCRs, roller coasters, CAT scans, washing machines, threshing machines, heart/lung machines, fax machines, refrigeration, plastics, telecommunications, electricity, pharmaceuticals, and lasers have contributed to easier, healthier, and longer lives.

Some of this technology, however, poses ethical dilemmas: How long do we leave patients on life-support machinery? What efforts should be made to save premature infants? How do we deal with the infirmities that increased life expectancy brings? Who has a claim on the limited supply of organs available for transplant? Should we develop technologies of war and destruction? Should we eliminate some microbes, such as the smallpox virus, which at present are deleterious but may in the future prove to have worth? Should we determine whether we possess genes that may result in incurable disease? What do we do if an ultrasound reveals a malformed fetus? What ethical parameters govern our use of technologies that are helpful to humans yet injurious to the environment? Can we justify the pain that our research inflicts on animals? Should spontaneously aborted fetuses be made available for research purposes or to supply materials useful in drug therapy? Can information systems be designed to protect personal privacy?

Some of the most difficult questions relate to work in genetics. Does manipulation of the human genome violate something sacred? In light of modern genetic engineering, how do we follow our charge to care responsibly for the created order and the dignity of human life?

A Historical Perspective

Ours is not the first generation that has been called upon to relate the Christian faith to scientific breakthroughs. The emergence of a scientific view of the world, in which immutable, rational, scientific law governs, challenged the Christian understanding of the purposeful action of God, God's miracles, and God's revelation. In many cases, Christians were able to expand their thinking, retreat from a theological arrogance, and discard their obsolete understandings of physical processes.

Others, however, resisted this new knowledge. When Copernicus (1473–1543) and then Galileo (1564–1642) suggested that geocentrism (the belief that the earth is the center of the solar system, as the Bible seemed to assume) was false, and that the sun was the center of the solar system (heliocentrism), some Christians felt that the credibility of scripture was threatened. As Robert M. Hutchins notes:

> The dissensions between Catholics and Protestants made both sects fearful of any scandal which might appear to undermine respect for the Church of the Bible, and consequently they became over-literal in their reading of Scripture and were inclined to condemn any assertion which could be construed as contradicting any literal interpretation of any passage in the Bible. Luther blustered that "the fool [that is, Copernicus] will upset the whole science of astronomy, but as the Holy Scripture shows, it was the sun and not the earth which Joshua ordered to stand still."[5]

Some responded similarly in the nineteenth century, when Charles Darwin postulated a mechanism, natural selection, that might explain both the variety and relatedness of life-forms. The conclusions that he drew from his and others' research challenged Christians' understanding of the creative process and required them to interpret the scriptural view of creation more figuratively, theologically, and critically, and less literally, historically, and scientifically.

In both these instances, some members of the church responded from a defensive position, with fear and foreboding, even anger. They were convinced that scripture had revealed all that they needed to know. They also assumed that the way they had always interpreted the scriptures was correct. To them, the Bible spoke literally and accurately to matters of science, even though it was written in a prescientific era.

These Christians vehemently resisted change. The image of a God who continues to reveal great and hidden things, who is actively at work in the world, who delights in sharing new truth, who is a God of wonder, who is consistent and never-changing yet capable of surprise, was new and even threatening.

The Church Today

As in the past, some Christians today may not be ready to reconsider their beliefs and theological positions. They may be wary of new ideas. They may fear what they deem to be heretical efforts to supplant their old beliefs. Some Christians have even suggested that too much knowledge can be a bad thing.

Francis Bacon in the seventeenth century was aware of our reluctance to reexamine beliefs and our resistance to anything that seems not to confirm our beliefs:

> The human understanding, when any proposition has been once laid down . . . forces everything else to add fresh support and confirmation; and although most cogent and abundant instances may exist to the contrary, yet either does not observe, or despises them, or it gets rid of and rejects them by some distinction, with violent and injurious prejudice, rather than sacrifice the authority of its first conclusions. (*Novum organum,* 1621)[6]

As Eric Hoffer notes, "No one really likes the new. . . . Even in slight things the experience of the new is rarely without some stirring or foreboding."[7] Vincent Ryan Ruggiero explains that change breaks routines, threatens established habits, challenges the familiar, and requires thinking, examining, and deciding. Many people find it easier just to think and act in old, comfortable ways.[8]

Horace T. Houf offers a similar assessment of those Christians who incline to holding older belief patterns and resist adapting to new realities:

> Their most natural and easy reaction to the present compli-
> cated situation, then, is to stand pat by the older standards
> of personal behavior and to suspect and reject the newer
> knowledge. This attitude easily wraps itself in the emotional
> halo of piety and devotion to the "good old past," its morals
> and its religion. While this attitude has reasons of its own
> and is comprehensible, it is not a possible or tenable way for
> the present generation, whose world is in many ways a new
> world which simply will not be thus set aside. The attitude
> here described is the obscurantist reaction, which tends to
> deny or resist all change and to make of morals and religion
> static phases of life, a position which more and more brings
> both morals and religion into disrepute and renders them in-
> adequate to present duties and needs.[9]

Anthropological research shows that change is hardest to accomplish in matters relating to the sacred.[10] Traditional practices are highly personal and emotional, involving cherished values and beliefs. They often endure long after they are instructive or relevant. Changes in scripture translations or hymnody often provoke discomfort, as do innovations in worship. It is not surprising that modification of biblical interpretation also meets resistance.

Yet a person who is unwilling or hesitant to consider new ideas or insights is not free to develop an attitude of informed skepticism, which questions past beliefs. Such a person cannot humbly admit to not having all the truth.

Such a mind-set fails to acknowledge this Creator as Lord of the universe. It seems to fear that God and God's Word might not be able to respond to the new challenges posed by scientific discovery. Not only has this attitude sometimes cost the church respect and credibility in the scientific community, it has also limited our understanding of the works of the God whom we profess to worship and whom we describe as sovereign, awesome, omnipotent, alive, active, Lord of all creation.

The Call to Develop Critical Thinking

How can the church be sure that its response to science is informed, thoughtful, and responsible, and that it honors God? How can we avoid knee-jerk reactions as science barrages us with new data, new interpretations of old data, new paradigms, and revolutionary ways of thinking? Along with undergirding our thoughts and convictions with prayer and an informed theology, we can develop and practice skills of *critical thinking.*

Critical thinking is often called higher order thinking, or just plain good or careful thinking. Its intellectual roots go back over two thousand years to Socrates. In more recent centuries, thinkers such as Voltaire, John Henry Newman, Immanuel Kant, John Stuart Mill, and William Graham Summer have further articulated Socrates' approach.[11]

Critical thinking is the responsible exercise of one of God's most amazing creations: the human mind. It is careful, thoughtful, courageous, and, above all, honest to God and honoring of God. It equips us to assess information accurately, arrive at appropriate conclusions, and defend them with clarity and humility. It is characterized by fairness, perseverance, intellectual integrity, humility, openmindedness, and rational self-criticism. It detects bias, recognizes prejudice, and sorts out relevant arguments. Critical thinkers think autonomously, or independently, and do not always believe what those around them believe.

We often believe ourselves to be objective, yet objectivity is quite rare, and irrationality and self-delusion are quite common. We do not always recognize when intuitive hunches, whims, customs, authoritative decrees, traditions, habits, instincts, or emotions are at work in our thinking. As William J. Reilly points out, "Although we can often see that the conclusions of another person are false, extravagant, prejudiced, or one-sided, each of us is inclined to feel that his own thinking is quite reasonable."[12]

Critical thinkers therefore inform themselves of all sides of a question. As John Stuart Mill stated, "The only way in which a human being can make some approach to knowing the whole of a subject, is by hearing what can be said about it by persons of every variety of opinion, and studying all modes in which it can be looked at by every character of mind."[13] According to Richard W. Paul,

> Critical thinkers recognize the importance of asking for reasons and considering alternative views. They are especially sensitive to possible strengths of arguments that they disagree with, recognizing the tendency of humans to ignore, oversimplify, distort, or otherwise unfairly dismiss them.[14]

Reilly has suggested the following rules:

1. Expose yourself to sources of evidence on all sides of the question.
2. Appraise the validity of your evidence from the standpoint of its source and the means used for gathering it.
3. Guard against the formation of opinion or premature judgments while in the process of examining evidence.
4. Keep the mind open and hospitable to new evidence on any side of the question.
5. Set up a balance sheet on each possible solution, stating your evidence for or against that course of action.
6. Weigh the relative importance of positive and negative evidence in each case.[15]

Developing an Appropriate Skepticism

People may develop an ability to assess a situation or various data quickly, and to draw appropriate and perceptive conclusions intuitively. Yet it should be noted that no one continuously and consistently employs critical thinking. To be open-minded, thorough, and unbiased in thinking is difficult.

As we have noted, the church has not always encouraged Christians to think for themselves, to question, to analyze, and to entertain opposing viewpoints. It is not uncommon to hear the word "indoctrinate" in church settings. Seekers are not always permitted to be questioners or doubters. If an authoritarian environment prevails, dialogue and alternative opinion will not have sufficient opportunity to flourish.

Interestingly, scientists have often had as much difficulty as others in switching belief paradigms and employing the objectivity and critical thinking that they have been taught. Darwin, in a particularly perceptive passage at the end of *The Origin of Species,* wrote:

> Although I am fully convinced of the truth of the views given in this volume . . . I by no means expect to convince experienced naturalists whose minds are stocked with a multitude of facts all viewed, during a long course of years, from a point of view directly opposite to mine. . . . But I look with confidence to the future—to young and rising naturalists, who will be able to view both sides of the question with impartiality.[16]

Thomas S. Kuhn relates how physicist Max Planck sadly remarked that "a new scientific truth does not triumph by convincing its opponents and making them see the light, but rather because its opponents eventually die, and a new generation grows up that is familiar with it."[17] Those who care about clear, honest, open-minded thinking must maintain constant vigilance.

Some educators suggest that critical thinking's most notable quality is skepticism, that is, an ability to ask appropriate and thoughtful questions.[18] Skepticism requires us to reserve judgment, sometimes indefinitely, until enough data are gathered to form a base for a belief or conclusion. Skeptics do not automatically jump on board or yield to the strong influence of unproved authorities.

Again, skepticism in some religious circles is equated with weak faith and questionable commitment. Individuals who are skeptical, who reserve judgment or question certain dogma, may be perceived as a threat to the status quo and established belief. Group disapproval and ostracism sometimes result.

Yet skepticism at its best contributes to increased insight and enlightenment, and protects us from quick, inaccurate, or unwise judgments. Moreover, it is not only analytical and cognitive, but also affective, that is, it has an emotional component. Critical thinkers appreciate creativity, are innovators, and exude a sense that life is full of possibilities. They see the future as open and malleable, not static, and have the self-confidence to change aspects of their world.[19] They are free to challenge old assumptions, explore and imagine alternatives, and assess new ideas, beliefs, or viewpoints.[20] They thirst for truth and radiate excitement.

Christians and Critical Thinking

Christ's teachings and life demonstrate that critical thinking honors God. The Gospels unremittingly emphasize the kind of change that allows us to grow in faith and love of God and each other. The term "repent" means "to turn around," to go in another direction. The apostle Paul repeatedly enjoins the readers of his letters to make changes in their attitudes, priorities, beliefs, behavior, and lifestyles.

Luke 10:25–37 records an example of critical thinking. A lawyer asked Jesus what he could do to inherit eternal life. Jesus referred him to the scripture: "What is written in the law? What do you read there?" A regular rabbinical formula was "What do you read?" But Jesus saw that the "how" was more important than the "what." As J. Carter Swaim notes,

> So on this occasion he is interrogating his inquisitor not merely about the contents of his reading but about the manner of it. Does he read in order to confirm his prejudices or to form his opinions? Does he read in order to confute his opponents, or to find out what and whom he ought to oppose? Does he read through the eyeglasses of tradition, everything colored by what the fathers taught, or does he read in the glad confidence that there is more light yet to break forth from God's holy Word?[21]

In Acts 8:30, Philip interrogates an official of the Abyssinian court who was reading the scroll of the prophet Isaiah. Philip was concerned that the content be clear. "Do you understand what you are reading?" We should ask these two questions, "What do you read there?" and "Do you understand what you are reading?" over and over as we read scripture, for critical thinking skills can aid, in fact are essential for, an accurate understanding of the Bible.

While we believe much by faith, we have ample opportunity and necessity to exercise the mind. Jesus challenged his listeners to "love the Lord your God with all your heart, and with all your soul, and with all your strength, and with all your *mind*" (Luke 10:27; emphasis added). Paul exhorted Timothy to attend to reading and doctrine (1 Timothy 4:13, 15–16; 5:17) and instructed Christians to think on what is true, honest, pure, and just (Philippians 4:8), to test all things (1 Thessalonians 5:21), and not to be children in their thinking (1 Corinthians 14:20). To the Romans, he said, "So then, with my mind I am a slave to the law of God" (7:25), and he challenged them to "put on the armor of light" (13:12). Similarly, Peter encouraged Christians to make every effort to add knowledge to their faith (2 Peter 1:5).

If ever Christians needed to exercise careful, responsible thinking, it is in the present era, with all of the enigmas and complexities of science. H. H. Lane, in 1923, exemplified well the lively thinking that Christians need today:

> The author has attempted to maintain the scientific attitude of mind, which consists in an honest endeavor to receive the truth whatever its nature and source, in a determination to secure all facts essential to the question at issue, with the intention of testing every hypothesis by application to further facts and relations, discarding each hypothesis whenever it becomes untenable by reason of contradictory phenomena, and of arriving at final judgments only when there seems no escape from them; in a spirit of tolerance for the opinions of others whether in accord or in disagreement with his own, a spirit which seeks to account for them rather than to ridicule or denounce them; in short, with a freedom from acrimony, blind partisanship and prejudice to seek the truth that makes men free.[22]

While God does not change, our ideas about God sometimes do. The Hebrews wrote about the God of the heavens, who came into the garden in the cool of the day, rested on the seventh day, made a rainbow to remind them of God's promise, smelled the sweet savor of burnt offerings, visibly appeared in a fiery furnace, and spoke out of a burning bush and whirlwind. Today we talk about the incarnate, transcendent, immanent, triune God: the God of the atom, DNA, radioactivity, plate tectonics, quarks, light years, and the Big Bang.

Similarly, while the scriptures are dependable and authoritative, our interpretation of them changes as our awareness of God's work in this world expands. Christians are continually challenged to interpret and apply the scriptures in light of what science reveals of God's amazing, dynamic creation. Many Christians are exhilarated by these disclosures and, like Piglet in *Winnie-the-Pooh,* they ask, "I wonder what's going to happen exciting *today?*"[23]

When Christians are open to understanding scientific data, they find new ways to interpret the perpetual and universal relevance of God's Word. They find that the creator God—changeless, dependable, and just, Rock and Anchor, mighty Fortress and never-failing Bulwark—can indeed surprise them, reveal novel concepts, freshly inspire awe, and challenge them to new heights of understanding. That God's ways are not our ways does not threaten them.

Some medical personnel and scientists, wisely acknowledging their limitations, are now inviting ethicists, chaplains, and theologians to assist them in making difficult ethical decisions about issues of genetic engineering. This opportunity to influence public policy is consistent with Jesus' charge to Christians to be light and salt in the world, providing illumination, direction, and vitality.

It is therefore imperative that the church stay informed about scientific research on human heredity and, where appropriate and necessary, be involved in shaping decisions that will affect individuals, future generations, and the created order. The moral principles of the Jewish and Christian scriptures can help to shape new guidelines, laws, and standards of value for the whole society.

NOTES

1. Johannes Kepler, *The Harmonies of the World,* as quoted in Robert M. Hutchins, ed., *Great Books of the Western World: Ptolemy, Copernicus, Kepler,* vol. 16 (Chicago: Encyclopaedia Britannica, 1952), 1080.

2. Cited in Albert N. Wells, "A New Openmindedness," in *The Christian Message in a Scientific Age* (Richmond, Va.: John Knox, 1962), 69.

3. Ibid., 67.

4. Ilya Prigogine, "The Rediscovery of Time," in *Science and Complexity,* ed. Sara Nash (Northwood, Middlesex: Science Reviews, 1985), 11.

5. Hutchins, 490.

6. As quoted in Michael J. Mahoney, *Cognition and Behavior Modification* (Cambridge, Mass.: Ballinger, 1974), 46.

7. Eric Hoffer, *The Ordeal of Change* (New York: Harper & Row, 1963), 1.

8. Vincent Ryan Ruggiero, *Beyond Feelings: A Guide to Critical Thinking* (Port Washington, N.Y.: Alfred Publishing Co., 1975), 59.

9. Horace T. Houf, *What Religion Is and Does* (New York: Harper & Bros., 1935), 55.

10. Goodwin Watson, "Resistance to Change," in *Creating Social Change,* ed. Gerald Zaltman, Philip Kotler, and Ira Kaufman (New York: Holt, Rinehart & Winston, 1972), 616.

11. Richard W. Paul, *Critical Thinking: What Every Person Needs to Survive in a Rapidly Changing World* (Rohnert Park, Calif.: Center for Critical Thinking and Moral Critique, 1990), 2. Aspects of this history will be explored in chapter 2 of this volume—Ed.

12. William J. Reilly, *The Twelve Rules for Straight Thinking* (New York: Harper & Row, 1947), 6.

13. As quoted in Paul, 10.

14. Ibid., 330.

15. Reilly, 101–104.

16. Charles Darwin, *The Origin of Species* (Cambridge, Mass.: Harvard University Press, 1964), 481–482.

17. Thomas S. Kuhn, *The Structure of Scientific Revolutions,* 2nd ed. (Chicago: University of Chicago Press, 1970), 151.

18. See John E. McPeck, *Critical Thinking and Education* (New York: St. Martin's, 1981), 6–7.

19. Stephen D. Brookfield, *Developing Critical Thinkers* (San Francisco: Jossey-Bass, 1987), 5.

20. Ibid., 11–12.

21. J. Carter Swaim, *Right and Wrong Ways to Use the Bible* (Philadelphia: Westminster, 1953), 16.

22. H. H. Lane, *Evolution and Christian Faith* (Princeton: Princeton University Press, 1923), 6.

23. A. A. Milne, *Winnie-the-Pooh* (New York: E. P. Dutton, 1926), 160.

Summary

Contemporary science and technology raise profound theological and ethical questions. The church will be able to make a creative contribution to their resolution only if it is willing to understand, and to think critically about, the new knowledge that lies behind them.

Critical thinking enables us to examine our assumptions, weigh different points of view, and seek a fuller understanding of the truth. We can open ourselves to new insights, are willing to change our minds in response to new information and evidence, and develop an attitude of informed skepticism.

At times, the church has resisted change. If we love God with heart, soul, and mind, however, we will embrace the search for truth. We will see the discoveries of science as a revelation of the breadth and depth of God's work.

Study Questions

1. How might God be revealing great and hidden things to us today?
2. What can the church learn from Christians' past responses to the revelations of science?
3. How should Christians today respond to the revelations of science?
4. What are some of the characteristics of critical thinking?
5. When should we be willing to change our beliefs? When not?
6. How does scripture encourage us to use our minds?
7. Is it a strength or a weakness to have a theology that invites us to interpret scripture in light of new insights from science?

Chapter 2

Singing the Lord's Song: Historical Interactions between Science and Religion

James B. Miller

A Place to Begin

By the rivers of Babylon—
there we sat down
and there we wept
when we remembered Zion.
On the willows there
we hung up our harps.
For there our captors
asked us for songs,
and our tormentors asked for mirth,
saying,
"Sing us one of the songs of Zion!"
How could we sing the LORD's song
in a foreign land?

(Psalm 137:1–4)

This plaintive opening to Psalm 137 expresses the religious anguish of a people whose theology had proven woefully inadequate. For centuries the people had proudly relied on the prophecy that the kingship of David and his heirs had been established forever.[1] Now

17

the kingdom had been overrun by the Babylonians, the temple built by Solomon had been destroyed, the line of Davidic kings had been broken, and a significant portion of the nation had been carried off into exile. The mocking of their captors made this national disaster all the more bitter. They called on the people of Israel to sing their triumphal "songs of Zion," songs of the Lord. Yet out of this experience of theological distress, a new theology, a theology of messianic hope, emerged.

We in North American mainline denominations live amid widespread theological discord, confusion, and pluralism today. To some, this state of affairs demonstrates that a secular culture has taken the church into exile. Others would argue that this exile is self-imposed, an exile into the ancient world of the Bible and away from the contemporary world. For still others, the present sense of uneasiness in the church arises from the apparent inability of the church to offer fitting theological and ethical insight into contemporary moral challenges, such as those posed by current developments in the biological sciences and their resulting technologies.

One source of the church's discomfort is its "Babylonian captivity" to a culture that has marginalized religion and separated theology from the main currents of intellectual life. It is ironic that Christians, especially Protestant Christians, both helped establish modern culture and acquiesced in their intellectual disestablishment by that culture. It is the intent of this chapter, however, to suggest that the theological distress of the present represents a call by God to the Christian community to rebuild Christian faith and Christian mission from their foundations, just as the Edict of Cyrus the Great liberated the people of Israel to return to their land to rebuild the temple.

Yet reconstruction of theological foundations is not common in the church today. Much of our theological reflection is what Reinhold Niebuhr called "applied Christianity." It is thinking about decision-making and action in the world. It is ethical thinking, thinking about what we as Christians ought to *do*. Such thinking assumes that a solid theological foundation already exists.

But it is just this assumption that needs to be reexamined. Classical and biblical worldviews have shaped traditional Christian theology. Since the sixteenth century, however, new understandings of the world have emerged. This more recent history has been largely "invisible" in the thought of the church.

There are two exceptions: the Copernican and Darwinian revolutions. Yet the church has diluted the significance of these two revolutions in Western thought. Theologians have generally failed to reconsider the theological geocentrism (earth-centeredness) that characterizes biblical thought. Further, those theologians who have been receptive to evolutionary theory have often assumed that human beings are exceptions to general evolutionary processes and have some extraordinary standing in the cosmic scheme of things.

In addition, the church's *theological* engagement of quantum physics and molecular biology, sciences that have come into being over the past hundred years, has been minimal. Churches have issued moral pronouncements on such varied topics as nuclear energy, medical technologies, and genetic experimentation, but the scientific understanding of the world that underlies these technological developments has been theologically "invisible."

Why Science Has Been Invisible to the Church's Theology

One reason for this "invisibility" is that the church, as part of its Babylonian captivity to the modern world, has accepted a division of the world into separate, impenetrable domains of the sacred and the secular, faith and fact, spirit and matter, the eternal and the temporal, religion and science/technology. At the same time, the church has maintained an implicit judgment that the domain of the sacred is more important, perhaps even more real, than that of the secular.

A second reason for the "invisibility" of science has been the philosophical "atrophy" of the church. From early in its history, the church actively participated in the development of Western thought.[2] Yet since the Enlightenment, much of the church has attempted to fence off a domain of intellectual turf that would be safe from the aggression of contemporary thinking. The church's lack of positive engagement with the intellectual struggles of the day has resulted in a diminished capacity for such struggle and in the church's virtual inability to reassess the foundations of its theology, including its assumptions about what the world is like. Perhaps, then, it is time to try to make the invisible visible, that is, to consider the worldviews in whose midst the church responds to God's call.

The history of Western culture can be fruitfully divided into three periods, each reflecting a distinctive worldview: the *Classical,* the *Modern,* and the *Emerging.*[3] The Classical period generated the issues from which the Modern period emerged, as has the Modern for the period that is now emerging. Moreover, as the Modern period transformed the way in which the world of the Classical period was understood, so also the Emerging view is transforming the Modern understanding.

Today, the church finds itself being whisked, perhaps against its will, out of a captivity to Modern culture to which it has accommodated itself. It is being required to reconstruct its theology, so that the new intellectual landscape can become "home." This is especially problematic because most of the church's theological symbols and concepts were forged against the backdrop of Classical culture. The church, like the Hebrews of the exile, finds that its traditional "songs" not only prompted derision in the context of Modern culture but are of questionable value for understanding the Emerging world of today. How did the church's historical journey lead to this state of affairs? We turn to the beginning of Western culture in the Classical world.

The Baptism of Aristotle: The Classical World[4]

The Classical world in the West emerged from the convergence of Greek ideas about the order and origin of the world and Hebraic theological understandings of the world as God's creation. In the century and a half before Socrates (470–399 B.C.), various movements in Greek philosophy proposed naturalistic, non-mythological, non-theistic explanations for the origin and structure of the cosmos.[5] These philosophies proposed developmental explanations for the origin of the world and life that were based not on acts of the gods but on the dynamic interactions of matter alone.

Pythagoras (580–500 B.C.) and his followers, who formed a kind of philosophical religious society, identified the order of the world with the order of numbers and geometric forms. Later Pythagoreans (for example, Aristarchus of Samos [ca. 310–230 B.C.]) even developed a model of the structure of the universe that assumed that the earth had a two-fold movement (both rotation and revolution) around a central celestial fire.[6] (It took another twelve centuries before this idea caught on!)

These pre-Socratic Greek worldviews contrasted with the theological account of the beginning of the universe found in the traditions of Israel. The mature form of Israel's view of the origin of the world is seen in the Priestly creation account (Genesis 1:1—2:4a). This worldview reflects the structural model of the world that prevailed broadly among Middle Eastern peoples in the thousand years prior to the origin of Christianity. But the people of Israel gave it a distinctive theological twist. For Israel, it was a world created not out of conflict and violence, as, for instance, in the Babylonian creation stories, but instead out of God's good pleasure. It was an intimate world in which God, the Creator of all, could walk in the garden in the cool of the day.

While the authors of Genesis expressed their theology of creation within a culturally shared cosmic framework, they did not speculate about the physical order of the world in any deliberate way. The Bible assumes and expresses the cosmic worldview of its time, but it does not theorize about it.

By the time of the birth of the Christian church, the philosophies of Plato (429–347 b.c.) and Aristotle (384–322 b.c.) had come to dominate Greek thought. Plato's worldview had a mythological element and included a creation story in which the world was made by a divine Creator in accordance with an ideal or perfect pattern. Many early Christian theologians found this philosophical creation story compatible with the Hebrew theological tradition. However, Plato's idealism (that is, his view that matter is less "real" and perfect than eternal immaterial ideas) seemed incompatible with the Hebrew tradition's unashamed affirmation of material existence.

In addition, the authors of the Hebrew scriptures made no fundamental distinction between the material and the immaterial. A human being was not an immortal soul captured in a material body, as Plato thought, but an enfleshed spirit. Because of this more holistic view, many early Christian theologians judged Aristotle's "realism" (that is, the view that things were a union of abstract form and concrete matter) to be more compatible with the Hebrew roots of Christian thought.

Although generalizations about the character of a cultural epoch must be tentative, it can be argued that the prevailing metaphor of the Classical world was an organic one. Plato understood the universe to be a single living organism. Aristotle, on the other hand, expressed his organic orientation in his understanding of the nature of causes. Though he held that there were four types of causes, he viewed final causality as the most fundamental.[7] Final causality was the causality of purpose, the type of causality most characteristic of the organic domain, the domain of life and intellect. It was also the type of cause most compatible with a purposeful Creator.

Building on this Greek tradition, the Egyptian astronomer Ptolemy (ca. 100–170) developed a complex geometric model of the universe based on the astronomical observations and geocentric theories of Hipparchus of Nicaea (160–125 B.C.), which were deeply rooted in Aristotle's philosophy. Ptolemy's Aristotelian geocentric model became the prevailing paradigm of the cosmos in Western, and particularly Christian, culture for more than a thousand years.

With the fall of the Roman empire, much of the learning of classical antiquity was lost in the West. But in the late medieval period a number of Christian theologians rediscovered Aristotle's philosophy.[8] The sources for this recovery included commentaries on Aristotle's works by Islamic and Jewish philosophers, newly commissioned translations of classical Aristotelian texts, and elements of Aristotle's philosophy that had already become embedded in the theological traditions of the church.[9] Thomas Aquinas adopted Aristotle's philosophy as the systematic intellectual framework within which to express the Christian faith. As a consequence, by the thirteenth century the creator God of the Hebrew tradition had become identical with the "unmoved mover" of Aristotelian cosmology. Due to this integration of natural philosophy and theology, Ptolemy's earth-centered model of the cosmos, based as it was upon Aristotle's philosophy, became the Christian cosmology.

On the eve of the birth of modern science, the relation between Aristotelian natural philosophy, Ptolemy's cosmic model, and Christian theology had become so tightly interwoven that it was virtually impossible to determine where one stopped and the other began. A philosophical challenge to Aristotle's philosophy of nature could hardly be seen as anything less than a challenge to theological ortho-doxy. The stage was set for the Copernican/Galilean controversy, out of which modern science emerged as a discipline that saw itself as in-dependent of the intellectual authority of ancient traditions, especially the traditions of the Christian church.

How the World Was Divided: The Rise of the Modern World

Along with the conflict over evolution, the Copernican/Galilean controversy is often cited as a prime example of the inevitable con-flict between religious dogmatism and rational inquiry. However, nei-ther Nicolaus Copernicus (1473–1543) nor Galileo Galilei (1564–1642) saw the issues as religious ones. Copernicus, it should be remem-bered, was a Polish Roman Catholic priest. Ironically, his work might never have been published if not for the enthusiastic urgings and as-sistance of two younger Lutheran scholars.[10]

Both Copernicus and Galileo understood quite clearly that they were challenging the prevailing philosophy (that is, Aristotelianism) of their day. Copernicus, however, escaped the controversy that was to rage around his theory because his revolutionary treatise did not ap-pear until near the time of his death.[11] It was Galileo who bore the brunt of the controversy.

Galileo was an Italian (and so nearer the center of Roman Catholic authority) and lived during a time in which the Protestant Re-formation had made more inroads into European society. His con-demnation, forced recantation, and house arrest must be understood more as products of the broader social struggle over authority (both political and religious) than as a consequence of a dispute between science and theology.[12] Be that as it may, the shift in cosmic vision begun by Copernicus and Galileo, a shift away from organic models emphasizing final causality to mechanical models emphasizing effi-cient causality described by mathematical laws of nature, helped ini-tiate an era in which the organic theological holism of the Classical period was torn apart.

The beginning of this era can also be associated with the work of the French mathematician and philosopher, René Descartes (1596–1650). Descartes is often identified as the father of Modern philosophy.

In 1619, Descartes had a profound religious experience in a series of dreams. He felt called to develop a new "universal science," one to replace the Aristotelian metaphysics of medieval scholasticism. In so doing, he helped initiate a fundamental split in the Western understanding of the cosmos.

For Descartes, reality was divided into two radically different domains: that of matter and that of mind (or spirit). The sciences were concerned with the former and developed rational mathematical and mechanical models to account for the behavior of material things. In the domain of mind or spirit, divine revelation and theological authority prevailed.

Throughout his career, Descartes tried in vain to determine how these two disparate substantial domains could be joined. This was for him a problem of philosophical anthropology, since humans were the only beings in which matter and spirit or body and mind converged. All other living things were simply complex machines. In seeking a solution, he suggested that the pineal gland was the physiological linchpin joining the mind with the body.

Although Descartes's mechanistic physics was largely set aside in favor of Isaac Newton's (1642–1727) later mathematical system, his metaphysical dualism of matter and spirit prevailed. It is said that Napoleon asked Pierre-Simon de Laplace (1749–1827), the French mathematical cosmologist and statistician who refined Newton's mechanics, about the place of God in his astronomical system. Laplace replied that he had no need of such a hypothesis. For him and his time, efficient or mechanical causes had become the sufficient means by which to explain the behavior of the material world.

A second defining characteristic of the Modern era was the rise of "critical" thought, usually associated with the philosophical works of Immanuel Kant (1724–1804). Kant's earliest writings were about the structure and origin of the universe; he proposed that the solar system had developed through the gravitational condensation of a cloud of cosmic dust. But Kant is best known for his analyses of human reason in his three "Critiques": *The Critique of Pure Reason, The Critique of Practical Reason,* and *The Critique of Judgment.*

Like Descartes, Kant divided the realm of knowledge into two fundamentally separate domains: that of the phenomena and that of the noumena. The phenomenal world is what we experience through our senses. But we do not experience the world directly. According to Kant, knowledge of phenomena, or what he meant by *knowledge* in the proper sense of the term, is formed by two elements: our contact with the world through our senses, and the active ordering of that sensory contact by the structure of our minds. This meant that one could not properly speak of knowing "things-in-themselves."

In contrast, the domain of the noumena consisted of things of which no sensory experience, and hence no knowledge, was possible, such as the universe as a causal whole, the human self as a free agent, and God. Yet in order for there to be science at all, it is necessary to believe that events have causes; in order for human activity to be held accountable to moral standards, it is necessary to assume the existence of a freely acting self; and in order for the world to be more than a mere aggregate of disparate objects and causal chains, it is necessary to affirm a perfect unifying principle for all existence, what Kant meant by God. Therefore, although Kant denied that one could know the world (as a causal network), the self, and God, he argued that faith in them was necessary for practical reasons. Descartes had divided reality into the realms of matter and spirit; Kant now divided it into the realms of pure and practical reason, of knowledge and faith, of empirical understanding and ethics, of science and religion. This dualism, along with that of Descartes, became the central mark of Modern culture. In many ways, it is still characteristic of contemporary culture.

There were a variety of theological responses to this broad cultural shift. At the turn of the nineteenth century, the Protestant theologian Friedrich Schleiermacher (1768–1834), who had diligently studied Kant's works, argued that religion was primarily a matter of feeling rather than reason, of the inner rather than the outer life, and of the subjective rather than the objective. His works provided the main foundations for what came to be called "liberal theology."

Neo-orthodox Christian theologies, both Protestant and Roman Catholic, developed in opposition to this theological liberalism.[13] Ironically, these new theologies were greatly influenced by Kantian thought. They tended to accept a division of knowledge between that derived through empirical observation (natural knowledge) and that received through divine revelation (supernatural, or transcendental, knowledge).

The Modern worldview continues to form the dominant perspective in contemporary Western and Christian culture. It is found in the popular understanding of science as an impersonal, detached, and objective search for the facts of nature and religion as an personal, involved, subjective commitment to values derived from supernature.

Yet the cultural authority of Modern thought and the Christian theologies to which it gave rise are on the wane. This decline is due, first, to developments from within the sciences that have transformed our understanding of the world and, second, to philosophical and theological reflections on their findings. The new Emerging era may be far from midday, but it is well past dawn.

Trouble at the Foundations: The Emerging World

Any attempt to characterize a historical period involves caricature. A period as rich in development as the past two centuries is especially hard to summarize. Moreover, to attempt to describe the defining features of a process of cultural change while it is still going on requires a certain amount of intellectual foolhardiness. Let me nonetheless offer what seems to be the broad shape of the worldview that is now coming into being around us.

Developments in biology and in physics have triggered the emergence of a fundamentally new cosmic vision. The prevailing images for the Classical world were organic. Those for the Modern world were mechanical and dualistic. The characteristic images for the Emerging world are historical, relational, and personal.

Nature Gains a Biography

With the rise of uniformitarian geology in the late eighteenth century and Darwin's evolutionary theory for biology in the nineteenth, the earth and all life upon it came to be seen not as unchanging parts of an inevitable plan but as historical products, formed as a consequence of particular events that could have occurred otherwise.[14] The world was no longer simply a given. It was a drama of creation and extinction, of the rise and fall of continents and species alike, of creative emergence and transformation. These historical processes continue and can be observed today.

In previous times it was believed that a thing was what it was because it embodied an eternal essence that determined its nature and value. In a world understood historically, one in which what a thing will become cannot be known until it actually becomes it, the idea of an eternal determining essence seems hard to justify.

Christian theology has affirmed that humans are distinguishable from the rest of nature by virtue of being created "in the image of God." However, from the point of view of evolutionary biology, humankind in its particular present form is the historical product of universal natural processes. Not only is nature historical but human beings are fully immersed in that history as both product and participant. Further, the evolutionary processes did not disappear when humans arrived on the scene. Evolution continues. The final chapters in the biography of nature and, in particular, the human species have yet to be written. It is very unlikely that the human species as we know it today will be present in the final chapter of the book of nature.

The Universe as Relative, Participatory, and Indeterminate

With Albert Einstein's (1879–1955) development of relativity physics, commonsense notions about space and time were abandoned. No longer can it be taken for granted that measurements of either distance or duration in one frame of reference will be identical to those taken in another. The motion of the reference frame affects measurement.

Although this idea does not accord with common sense, it has been demonstrated in an experiment with two very accurate atomic clocks. After being set at the same time, one was placed at the center of a large turntable and the other at the turntable's rim. The turntable was then rotated at a rapid speed. The clock on the rim had a velocity greater than the clock at the center. After a long period of time, the turntable was stopped and the two clocks were compared. The one on the rim had run slower than the one at the center of the turntable.

Further, Einstein's General Theory of Relativity proposed a different understanding of gravity. Newton had understood gravity to be a mysterious machine-like force operating at a distance. He would not speculate about what it was and was satisfied simply to describe it mathematically. Einstein, however, proposed that gravity should be understood as an acceleration caused by the curvature of space/time due to the mass of an object. Mass tells space/time how to curve, and space/time tells mass how to move. Gravity should be understood as a relationship rather than as a force.

Finally, when Einstein, Nils Bohr (1885–1962), Werner Heisenberg (1901–1976), and others developed quantum theory to describe the behavior of the smallest constituents of the world, the commonsense notion that we live in a world comprised of separate distinct things became highly suspect. Although contemporary physicists use "particle" language to describe the extremely small entities that they investigate, these entities are not what we would ordinarily call little bits of stuff.

In one respect, "particle" language is inadequate because some subatomic entities display wave-like as well as particle-like behavior. But whether we use "particle" or "wave" language, we could still be tempted to ask, "Particles of what? Waves of what?" Of what ultimate stuff is the cosmos composed? The answer from quantum physics seems to be, "Nothing" (or, perhaps more precisely, "No-Thing"). At its most fundamental level, the universe does not seem to be composed of stuff or things at all but instead of dynamic relating.

As quantum theory developed, it became evident that certain characteristics of the entities being investigated were coupled in such a way that to determine one characteristic with increasing accuracy was to disable one's ability to determine the other—what Heisenberg expressed as the "principle of uncertainty." It is important to emphasize that this "uncertainty" is not the result of clumsy instruments or inadequate observational techniques. Instead, it seems that at the core of reality there is an uncertainty (or indeterminacy) that no amount or quality of observation can overcome. This conclusion runs sharply counter to the Modern presupposition that the world is, in principle, open to full and complete description. It suggests, instead, that an unfathomable mystery lies at the core of reality.

Another consequence of the development of quantum physics has to do with the issue of objectivity. From the Modern perspective, the sciences deal with objective knowledge that derives from detached impersonal observation of the facts of nature. Contemporary physics, however, has effectively shown that, while there can be a relative objectivity in the practice of science (that is, one based upon the adherence of the individual scientist to a set of standards and procedures accepted by the scientific community), there is no observation in which the object observed and the subject observing are absolutely separate. That is to say, there are no facts in nature independent of some particular observer. To paraphrase one contemporary philosopher of science, nature must be allowed to answer for herself, but it is always we who ask the questions. And the form of the questions determines to a significant degree the kind of answers we receive.

In summary, the development of evolutionary theory in biology and of relativity and quantum theories in physics has led to a vision of the universe not as a thing that has a history, but as history itself. The cosmos has come to be seen not as a system of independent atomic parts linked together by external mechanical forces but, instead, as a dynamic nexus of relatings. In such a universe, particular parts (things) do not exist independently but are constituted by shifting internal relations within an ever-changing whole.

From Science to Philosophy

The shift in worldview that has been spurred by such findings in the sciences has been accompanied by a variety of developments in philosophy. These developments also have significance for contemporary Christian theology and ethics.

Meaning as a Matter of Context

Ludwig Wittgenstein (1889–1951) was trained to be an engineering scientist. But as his life developed, he was drawn almost compulsively to questions about the logic of relations, and especially about the logic of language.

At first, Wittgenstein tried to develop a theory of language as arising out of logical relations. Yet he recognized that what seemed most important in human life (for example, issues of value) stood beyond the ability of logic to describe. So, he was very suspicious of philosophical systems that claimed to give a definitive, authoritative, or final, logical description of the totality of existence.

Wittgenstein finally concluded that language was best understood not in terms of a formal logic but rather as a form of human activity ("a game") in support of a set of human purposes ("a form of life"). The significance of a particular language game (for example, science) was not that it captured a picture that conformed to reality but instead that it served to support the achievement of certain ends. This contextual understanding of language sharply undercut the viewpoint (whether in science, philosophy, or theology) that language can have absolute (or non-contextual) meaning.

Knowledge as Evolutionary

Philosophers of science like Karl Popper, Thomas Kuhn, and Stephen Toulmin have offered careful analyses of the general features of actual scientific practice. Popper showed how science is not simply a logical enterprise but ultimately depends upon the alogical creative exercise of human imagination in order to generate its theories. Kuhn pioneered the analysis of science as a historical phenomenon in which fundamental shifts in theory are not simply logical modifications or reinterpretations of past knowledge, but are instead radical transformations of worldview—what he called "paradigm shifts."

Toulmin moved beyond both Popper and Kuhn. On the one hand, he was critical of Popper's tendency to over-rationalize human knowledge by proposing rational criteria to distinguish science from pseudo-science. On the other hand, he was critical of Kuhn's tendency to over-relativize knowledge as, for example, when Kuhn argues that there is no connection between earlier and later paradigms. In contrast to both, Toulmin proposed that human knowing should be understood as an evolutionary or ecological process paralleling what is found in biology. Knowledge, for Toulmin, exhibits a dynamism in which newer views emerge out of older ones, some older ideas simply become extinct, and human reason is grounded more in intentions or purposes than in logic.

Knowledge as Personal

Michael Polanyi, a Hungarian physical chemist who also began his philosophical reflections by focusing on scientific practice, showed that the Modern distinction between objective and subjective knowing is illusory. For Polanyi, all knowing is best categorized as personal, that is, all knowing is dependent upon the commitment of the knower within a community of shared values. Further, Polanyi showed how all knowledge that could be expressed in language was inherently dependent upon knowledge that was tacit, that is, either unexpressed or inexpressible. Thus, while he affirmed that we often say more than we know that we say, he argued that it was equally true (and perhaps more significant) that we know more than we *can* say.

What does this mean exactly? The easiest examples are found in the area of skills knowledge. Have you ever tried to explain to someone how to ride a bicycle? No amount of words is able to convey the complex sensory/motor relationships that must be exercised in order to balance on a two-wheeler. Only by climbing on the bike and experiencing what is needed (and sometimes by falling off) can a person learn to ride. In a similar fashion, an intern cannot be taught by language alone all the knowledge that is required in order to become a skilled diagnostician. It is only by making rounds, by observing an already skilled physician diagnose illness, and by attempting diagnoses under the eye of a competent diagnostician that the novice gains the tacit knowledge needed to unify the explicit knowledge of medical tests and measurements into an accurate diagnosis.

A common characteristic of those who have helped form the Emerging perspective is a skepticism about philosophical efforts to build systems that claim to describe fully the nature of reality. In the past, philosophers concerned with metaphysics (and especially the second and third generation disciples of the most original thinkers) have often exhibited gross intellectual pride. But does skepticism about such claims mean that in the Emerging world metaphysics must be abandoned? Does it mean that we can have no general or unifying systems to describe what is real? If the only choice is to choose between various assertions of reality, then the answer would have to be, "Yes." But this is not the only choice. Among the speculative philosophers of this century there is at least one who displayed a remarkable modesty with respect to the results of his own reflection.

The Cosmos as History

Late in his life Alfred North Whitehead (1861–1947) instructed his wife that upon his death his unpublished papers should be destroyed. He did not want those who followed him trying to decipher the meaning of his unfinished work when they needed to be doing original work of their own.

Whitehead's philosophical modesty was perhaps an outgrowth of his own intellectual experience. His early academic career focused on problems in the logic of mathematics. In partnership with Bertrand Russell (1872–1970) he attempted to describe the logical foundations of mathematics. The result, *Principia Mathematica* (published between 1910–1913), was an extraordinary example of logical analysis and system building. In 1931, however, mathematician Kurt Gödel demonstrated that no such system could be both logically consistent and complete.[15] Such a devastating critique might have crushed another scholar. Yet even before Gödel's proof, Whitehead, with characteristic modesty, had turned his attention to broader, more speculative philosophical concerns.

Even if modest, Whitehead's philosophical agenda was a bold one; namely, to propose an alternative to the speculative cosmology that had dominated Western thought for over two thousand years. As noted earlier, the vision that has been emerging from contemporary science imagines the cosmos as history rather than as a thing that has a history. In *Process and Reality,* Whitehead presented a comprehensive description of reality not in terms of things but in terms of events (that is, temporal units of relatedness or what he called "actual occasions"). Because Whitehead's thought included an explicitly theological element, it has stimulated a variety of efforts to reconsider the doctrinal affirmations of the Christian heritage in relation to this understanding of the world.[16]

The Lord's Song Reprise: A Call for Composers

Hutton and Lyell, Darwin, Einstein and Bohr and Heisenberg, Wittgenstein, Popper and Kuhn and Toulmin, Polanyi, and Whitehead—

these are but some of the voices that have been providing a melody for a song that expresses a new, emerging way of apprehending the world. We in the church have at least three responses from which to choose.

First, we can sing our own song, one that is different from all others in the world, whether of the sciences, philosophy, or the other great world religious traditions. This choice would require us to isolate and insulate ourselves from other singers, so that our voices do not contribute to a cacophony of noise that in the end would be no singing at all. But if we choose to be alone in our singing, why should we expect other singers in the Emerging world to join their voices with ours, to share our song, or even to listen to our song?

Second, we could require all other singers in the world, whatever the distinctive melodies that spring from their own context and experience, to sing only our song. We could claim that ours is the only genuine song, so that all who would be real singers must sing it. But our song by itself, even when sung by a multitude, lacks the rich range of possible harmonies that can be heard in relation to other songs in the world. A great chorus in which all the voices sing the same notes in the same rhythm lacks the fullness and richness of even a quartet singing in four parts with a syncopated rhythm.

Finally, we could seek that song whose harmony is the richest union of the lines of melody contributed by all the singers of the world. This, I would suggest, is the Lord's song. It is a song that takes seriously the authenticity of all the songs, whether the singer be a scientist or philosopher or artist or Hindu or Native American. It is a song that remembers and draws upon ancient songs carried forward from the tradition while discovering new harmonics never before heard. It is a song that resolves melodic difference as harmonic contrast rather than as discordant dissonance. It is with enlivening passion that the church needs to compose its own authentic melodic line for such a song in the strange land of the Emerging world. It is to be such composers that God is calling the church today.

NOTES

1. See 2 Samuel 7:4–17.

2. While Tertullian (160–230) made a sharp division between the life of faith and the explorations of reason, Origen of Alexandria (185–254), Augustine of Hippo (354–430), John Philoponus (490–556), Albertus Magnus (1193–1280), and Thomas Aquinas (1225–1274) are but a few of those within the church who contributed to the shaping of the Western mind.

3. It is difficult to know what to call this third period. My personal inclination is to call it the Postmodern/Post-Critical period (or Postmodern, for short). But the expression Postmodern has become much disputed, and so I have chosen the somewhat awkward term Emergent, or Emerging.

4. One might be surprised to learn how many university students take this title literally, in spite of the fact that Aristotle died over three hundred years before Jesus was born!

5. The leading figures in these movements were Anaximander (610–546 B.C.), the Atomists, and Epicurus (342–270 B.C.). The Atomists gave us the word "atom," which in Greek means "least divisible part." They are exemplified by Democritus (460–362 B.C.) and Leucippus (5th century B.C.). The Atomists proposed a materialist, non-theological cosmology in which all existing things were composed of combinations of atoms of varying shapes and textures and the void (or emptiness).

6. This "central celestial fire" was not initially identified as the sun. It was said that it was never visible from the inhabited regions of the earth because the uninhabited region of the earth was always facing this fire. In order for one body revolving around another to keep one side always pointed toward the other, it must make one full rotation on its axis in the same amount of time it takes to go around the other (as the moon does in relation to the earth).

7. Formal causes of the behavior of an object are those associated with its form or shape; material causes are those associated with the material composition of the object; efficient or mechanical causes are those that occur due to the direct impact of objects upon one another; final causes are goals toward which an object moves or develops.

8. For example, Bonaventure (1221–1274) and Thomas Aquinas (1225–1274).

9. See the Muslim Ibn Rushd (1126–1198), and the Jew Moses ben Maimon (1135–1204).

10. Georg Joachim Rheticus (1514–1576) and Andreas Osiander (1498–1552).

11. In a preface to Copernicus' book, Osiander, in an effort to circumvent controversy, claimed that the book offered not a true description of the world, but rather a better way of calculating the positions of the planets and stars.

12. In addition, the conflict was fueled by Galileo's own aggressive character and incisive wit. His *Dialogue on the Two Great World Systems* contributed to his downfall by putting the words of the Pope in the mouth of a fool.

13. See the Protestant theologian Karl Barth (1886–1968) and the Roman Catholic theologian Karl Rahner (1904–1984).

14. Uniformitarian geology held that the present shape and structure of the earth were the result of ordinary natural forces (wind and rain, erosion, sedimentation, volcanic eruption, etc.) acting over long periods of time. The Scotsman James Hutton (1726–1797) and the Englishman Charles Lyell (1797–1875) pioneered this position.

15. This finding for logical systems seems to be the equivalent of Heisenberg's "principle of uncertainty" and of Polanyi's understanding of the tacit foundation of all explicit knowing.

16. See John B. Cobb's *A Christian Natural Theology* (1965), Ian Barbour's *Religion in an Age of Science* (1990), Sallie McFague's *The Body of God* (1993), and Jack Haught's *Science and Religion: From Conflict to Conversation* (1995). Protestant theologians who do not draw upon a Whiteheadian metaphysical framework but have sought to rearticulate Christian theology in the light of the findings of science include Thomas Torrance, Jürgen Moltmann, and Wolfhart Pannenberg.

Summary

For the most part, the church has failed to engage contemporary developments in science. It has withdrawn into its own life, rather than interpreting the new intellectual movements of our day.

The church played a different role in the Classical world. The effort to use the Greek philosophical tradition (the Classical worldview) to express the Christian faith resulted in some of the church's greatest theological achievements. At the time of the Enlightenment, however, a broad cultural shift took place. Western philosophical thought sought to free itself from the church and its authority. The legacy of Descartes and Kant divided reality into two realms: matter and spirit, knowledge and faith, science and religion. Even as it reacted against aspects of the Enlightenment, the church tended to accept this division (the Modern worldview).

Contemporary developments in biology and physics signal yet another cultural shift. The fundamental categories for understanding reality are now historical, relational, and contextual. The idea that knowledge is always partial and influenced by the stance of the observer has replaced the notion of objective knowledge. The cosmos itself is understood to be in constant flux (the Emergent worldview).

The church is now challenged to relate its theology to this new understanding of the world—not to retreat, not to succumb, but to find its own voice, so that it can contribute to a richer understanding of the world.

Study Questions

1. What are some of the basic characteristics of each of the periods that Miller identifies (the Classical, the Modern, and the Emergent)?
2. Some philosophers and theologians have argued that the shift from the Modern to the Emergent (or Postmodern) period offers more favorable circumstances for the church to raise a public voice. What in the Modern period encouraged the church to accept a place in the private realm? What in the Emergent period might call the church back into the public realm?

3. How should the church respond to the intellectual claims of the Emergent period? Does the Emergent worldview help us to understand better the character of God and of our life before God? Or does the Emergent worldview undercut the church's claim to know something of the truth about God and God's ways?

Chapter 3

Genesis 1: A Song of Praise to the God of All Creation

James Ayers

How We Read

Before we consider how we might read Genesis 1, let us take a moment to consider how we read other things. Suppose you turn the page of your newspaper and encounter a Peanuts comic strip, one that begins with Snoopy sitting on top of his dog house, pretending he is a World War I flying ace. In succeeding panels he sits in a French café, drinks his mug of root beer, and flirts with his imaginary waitress.

You read a daily paper, we will propose, because you want to keep up on current events. You expect to find reports on such events in your newspaper. Yet you do not consider this depiction of Snoopy to report current information about the inner thoughts of an actual beagle. Why not? Because your extensive experience as a reader of newspapers equips you to recognize, without conscious deliberation, the difference between a news report and a comic strip.

Indeed, given a set of unlabeled excerpts, each perhaps half a dozen lines long, from (1) a news story, (2) an editorial, (3) an advice column, and (4) the want ads, most habitual newspaper readers would be able to identify which was which in only a moment. Each of these different types or genres of newspaper writing has its own style, and the experienced reader recognizes them without effort. Only the clumsiest of readers would take the Peanuts strip to be a news report about canine psychology.

Or consider a congregation singing out with gusto, "Mine eyes have seen the glory of the coming of the Lord, he is trampling out the vintage where the grapes of wrath are stored." None of us feels at that moment that we are being fundamentally dishonest, even though we have not, in fact, seen God trampling on grapes of wrath. Perhaps we just sing, and let the music carry us along. Or, if we think about what we are singing, we recognize that the hymn is a song of praise about God's righteous judgment. Only in the most metaphorical sense can it be called a description of what our eyes have seen. But that is all right. Only the clumsiest of observers would suppose that the singers have physically viewed a particular sight.

Consider a mother telling her children to finish their assigned tasks. They are dawdling. She becomes frustrated, and says, "I've told you a million times, you won't get your allowance if you don't get your chores done on time." Even very young children quickly understand that her statement is not about counting how many times she has given that warning. Only the clumsiest of observers would offer a mathematical demonstration that the number of warnings is much less than a million.

We are quite adept at recognizing the different genres of English speech and writing, for we encounter them all the time. But we are often not so adept when it comes to reading the Bible.

First, the language that we encounter in newspapers and in conversation surrounds us daily. We are in the midst of it continually. But the languages of the Bible, Hebrew and Greek, are foreign and ancient. They reflect cultures that are very different from our own. Even the most dedicated scholars remain unsure of the meaning of some of the more obscure words and phrases.

Second, not only do we start with much less knowledge of the culture and language of the Bible, but we also spend most of our time getting better at learning our own language and culture. All day long we engage in tasks that keep our English language skills sharp. We do not invest nearly that much time in scripture. Even among those who argue that the Bible is the absolute authority for the

Christian, few spend as much as an hour a day reading and study-ing it.

Third, our common usage of English is interactive. If we are not quite sure what someone means by a given comment, we can usually speak up and ask for clarification. To dig into a Bible passage in quest of better understanding is time- and labor-intensive compared to the moment or two it takes to ask a follow-up question in a classroom or a conversation.

For these three reasons, then, we may be clumsy readers of the Bible. Also, much of our difficulty in understanding scripture can be traced to the mistaken notion that whatever we read in scripture is a straightforward reporting of fact.

We do not speak modern English in that way, nor is it the way people spoke in the Bible. In this chapter, I will show, first, that there is little basis for reading Genesis 1 as if it were a newspaper story re-porting on events that took place during a certain week of the history of the world, and second, that there is a wealth of evidence that we should take it, instead, to be a hymn of praise.

Much of the conflict between faith and science is a result of the notion that astronomy and biology report one method of the devel-opment of the solar system and life on earth, and Genesis another. I hope to persuade you that my quest to reconcile these two is not a case of special pleading and does not require serious twisting of ei-ther science or scripture.

Is Genesis 1 Historical Reporting?

There is plenty of historical reporting in the Bible. An obvious ex-ample is the first chapter of Galatians, where Paul tells part of his biog-raphy. Another example is the opening verses of Luke and Acts, which state the author's intention to provide a careful report of specific events. At times, the biblical authors explicitly indicate that they were present when the events took place (one notes, for example, the transition from "they" language to "we" language in Acts 16:6–12, or how Nehemiah gives us his own story of what happened to him). At other times, the author was not present, and must write the history relying on a report given by someone else. The point is: reporting requires a reporter.

Who reported the events in Genesis 1? Nowhere does the book of Genesis give the name of an author. And nowhere does it indicate any source for a historical report of the creation of the world.

Let us assume for a moment that Moses was the author of the book of Genesis, perhaps in his free time during the evenings, while the children of Israel were wandering in the desert after the Exodus but before entering the promised land. We can thereby set a date for the writing of Genesis as approximately 1300 B.C. According to the dating system developed by Archbishop James Ussher (1581–1656) and made popular in America by the Scofield Reference Bible, the week of creation described in Genesis 1 took place in 4004 B.C., roughly twenty-seven centuries before the time of Moses.

If we take Genesis 1 as a historical report written down by Moses, we clearly cannot claim that Moses was an eyewitness to the events that he relates. Yet historical reporting requires a reporter. What reporter could Moses turn to for information on what was going on twenty-seven centuries before he lived?

A useful comparison can be made by asking, "What do we know about what was happening in Patagonia twenty-seven centuries ago in the year 700 B.C.?" Not too much. We can piece together a few general trends about economy, music, and culture, but can say little about actual events from that era. What do we know, in comparison, about what was going on in Jerusalem in the year 700 B.C.? Quite a bit, relatively speaking. We have extensive written records from people who lived in that era, and archaeologists have been able to uncover much supplemental information. Historians can, with due caution, write about what was happening at the end of the eighth century B.C. in Jerusalem.

Moses would have been in the same position that we are in with regard to Patagonia. He would have had no reporter to provide him information about what was happening twenty-seven centuries earlier. Perhaps someone will suggest that Moses had an extraordinary source of knowledge: God. Yet there is no description anywhere in the Bible of an occasion when God gave Moses a report of what happened at creation.

One might also try to justify this viewpoint on the basis of the following syllogism:

All the writing in the Bible is factual reporting of events.

Genesis 1 is a piece of writing in the Bible.

Therefore Genesis 1 is a factual reporting of events.

If we accepted the soundness of this reasoning, we would have to concede that we do not know how Moses found out the details of these events. We simply know that somehow he must have.

But this will not do. As we have seen, there certainly is factual reporting of events in the Bible. Yet there are many other kinds of writings as well: parables, poems, prayers, songs of desolation and songs of rejoicing, even an occasional fable (Judges 9:8–15). There is no way to justify the claim of the syllogism's major premise, that is, that all the writing in the Bible is factual reporting of events. And therefore there is no way to conclude from that claim that Genesis 1 is a factual report.

Still, does not Genesis 1 present itself as straightforward reporting of how creation took place? No, it presents itself as a poem, with six stanzas.

Genesis 1 as Poetry

In English, poetry, whether recited or sung, has certain characteristics, such as rhyme and meter:

> Listen, my children, and you shall hear
> Of the midnight ride of Paul Revere
> On the eighteenth of April, in '75.
> Hardly a man is still alive
> Who remembers that famous day and year.

Or:

> Hark, the herald angels sing,
> "Glory to the newborn king.
> Peace on earth, and mercy mild
> God and sinners reconciled."

The primary identifying characteristic of poetry in Hebrew is parallelism. Parallelism is a way of rhyming ideas, rather than the sounds of the words. Here are some representative verses from Psalm 91:

1 You who live in the shelter of the Most High,
   who abide in the shadow of the Almighty

4 He will cover you with his pinions,
   and under his wings you will find refuge.
   His faithfulness is a shield and buckler.

7 A thousand may fall at your side,
   ten thousand at your right hand,
   but it will not come near you.

The first line of verse 1 has three elements, each of which is explicitly paralleled in the second line: "You who live" is paralleled by "who abide," "in the shelter" by "in the shadow," and "of the Most High" by "of the Almighty."

We do not always find this level of exactness in the parallelism. The first line of verse 4 has two elements. "He will cover you" is paralleled by "you will find refuge," and "with his pinions" by "under his wings." It is interesting that the order of these elements is reversed in the second line. Moreover, the subject of the verb is God in the first line, but is the reader in the second line.

In verse 7, the verb is not repeated but is simply understood: "Ten thousand *may fall* at your right hand." And the final line of both verse 4 and verse 7 carries the idea of the preceding lines a bit further, without being synonymous to them.

At times, Hebrew poetry uses opposites. Here are several representative samples from the book of Proverbs.

A gossip goes about telling secrets,
   but one who is trustworthy in spirit keeps a confidence.
(11:13)

The wise are cautious and turn away from evil,
   but the fool throws off restraint and is careless.
(14:16)

The key characteristic of Hebrew poetry, then, is parallelism. Various elements in one portion are paralleled by elements in the next. These elements can be synonymous, or they can be opposites, or they can carry the thought on to the next step. Once a person becomes accustomed to this characteristic, the parallelism of structure in Hebrew poetry becomes quite obvious.

Do we see anything like this in the first chapter of Genesis? I would propose that with even this limited background in the nature of Hebrew poetry, a reader will immediately see that Genesis 1 is full of deliberate, explicit parallelism. It is unmistakably designed as a poem, and indeed as a hymn of praise.

If, for the sake of convenience, we call each of the days of creation a stanza, we will see that nearly every stanza contains the following elements:

God said, "Let . . ." such-and-such be the case.
And it was so.
God saw that it was good.
There was evening and there was morning, the *Nth* day.

In the first three stanzas, God calls things by name. This feature is absent in the second three stanzas; instead, they include the idea that God gives authority to one of the elements whose creation has been mentioned in that stanza. The sun, moon, and stars of stanza four are to rule over the day and the night, and are to be for signs and seasons and days and years. The creatures of the sea and sky are commissioned to fill the water and the air. The humans are given dominion over the earth.

In sum, then, in the first trio of stanzas, three different realms are created. In the following three, rulers of those realms are created and appointed to their positions in those realms.

Realms	*Rulers*
Day 1	Day 4
Light and darkness	Light bearers
Day 2	Day 5
Sea and sky	Sea and sky creatures
Day 3	Day 6
Land	Land creatures, humans

In addition to the way that all the stanzas parallel each other, there is a parallelism among the first three (calling things by name) and among the last three (giving things authority). There is also a parallelism across the trios: between Day 1 and Day 4, Day 2 and Day 5, Day 3 and Day 6.

What all this suggests is that Genesis 1 is a carefully constructed hymn of praise to God, the Creator of all that is. The writer of this hymn of course had no personal knowledge of how creation actually took place or over what time span, for the point of the hymn is not to give particular information about particular processes, but to offer up a grateful declaration of love, admiration, and worship to God.

This intent is, perhaps, a bit more obvious in Psalm 8:

When I look at your heavens, the work of your fingers,
the moon and the stars that you have established;
what are human beings that you are mindful of them,
mortals that you care for them?

While watching a sunset or gazing at the starry night in the mountains or at the seashore, we have all had the experience of how small humans are compared to the immense creation in all its grandeur. Psalm 8 speaks to this sense of wonder by using a particular metaphorical framework: it describes the moon and the stars as the work of God's fingers. A clumsy observer might argue on the basis of the psalm that God has fingers and that the stars are God's needlework, embroidered on the fabric of the sky. But that would be, once again, an instance of supposing that everything in the Bible is a report of events, instead of recognizing that songs utilize metaphorical frameworks of various kinds. We recall that "Mine eyes have seen the glory" is not about God trampling grapes in a winepress, even though it uses that metaphorical framework. Nor is Psalm 8 about God's fingers or God's fingerwork; instead, it uses that metaphorical framework to talk about the awe that we humans experience. Against the reaches of the stars we seem quite insignificant, for the vast night sky is just detail work to God—and yet God loves us.

This sense of wonder and worship is the theme of many hymns, ancient and modern.

> For the beauty of the earth,
> For the beauty of the skies,
> For the love which from our birth
> Over and around us lies:
> Lord of all, to Thee we raise
> This our hymn of grateful praise.

And that is what Genesis 1 is about, too. It is a song offered in worship to God, who has entrusted so much beauty and blessing into human hands. It is constructed within a particular metaphorical framework: a week of work that ends in a sabbath. Is the point of such a song to instruct us on the details of the metaphorical framework? Is it the purpose of Genesis 1 to teach us, for example, that there was sufficient light to grow green plants on day 3, even though the sun would not be created until day 4? Surely not. Instead, the point of the hymn is to give us words to sing of the power and majesty of the Lord who has created all that is.

That interpretation works if we allow the text of Genesis 1 to speak for itself. We allow the parallel elements that have been carefully crafted into each stanza to have their rightful authority in instructing us how to hear the hymn of praise that we find there.

Singing the Hymn of Praise in Genesis 1

The fact that hymns do not function in the same way as news reports does not mean that hymns have no content. When the congregation sings "Mine eyes have seen the glory," we do not conclude that the singers have seen God trampling on grapes of wrath. But we also should not conclude that the song means nothing at all.

In "Mine eyes have seen the glory," for example, the hymn speaks of God's great searching righteousness, and of God's action to establish that righteousness in human hearts. The singers exhort one another to give themselves to fulfill God's righteous purpose: "O be swift, my soul, to answer him! Be jubilant, my feet!" And to do so even at great cost to themselves: "As he died to make men holy, let us die to make men free."

If Genesis 1 is a hymn of praise to the Creator, what does it mean to sing that hymn? Let me suggest four themes.

First, the creation is good. This refrain runs throughout the hymn. The hymn does not spell it out, nor should we expect it to. Instead, the goodness of creation is simply there. It is a solid, recurring theme, a foundational fact to be seen wherever we turn our eyes.

Second, God is majestically sovereign over all creation. God speaks, and it is so. No explanation is given of what process will be used. No span of time is indicated for things to come into being. Many have therefore supposed that there was neither process nor time span. Yet that is surely too large a conclusion to draw. (We might compare Genesis 18:10, where God says that Sarah will have a son. No process is mentioned there either, yet presumably she gave birth as all mothers do.) What the hymn celebrates and affirms is God's sovereignty. The means by which that sovereign power brings things into being is simply not discussed.

If the ancient hymn writers had understood what we today understand of physics, astronomy, and biology, they would perhaps have discussed the means by which God brought the universe and life into being. Or perhaps not. They might not have thought that kind of discussion belonged in the setting of a hymn.

We should therefore not assume that this hymn is simply a reflection of their ignorance. We may understand certain processes better than the ancients did, yet we should feel equally confident that much of our knowledge will look simplistic centuries from now. Indeed, even within our present state of knowledge, we must frequently concede that we do not know the answer to various vexing questions. Even if the mysteries that baffled people of ancient times are not the same as those that baffle us, we continually encounter new unsolved problems.

To admit the mystery of God's ways is not to assert that when no scientific explanation is presently available for how something takes place, we should simply shrug and say, "God does it, by divine power." Rather, it is to ascribe confidence in God's sovereignty over all creation, no matter how far beyond our capability an explanation may be at any given moment in the history of science.

Third, humans have a role within creation. God speaks to the humans and gives them instructions. The instructions are brief: "Be fruitful and multiply . . . and have dominion over" the various animals

(Genesis 1:28). Much biblical commentary and theological analysis has been written about the nature of the "dominion" that humans are to exercise. Because Genesis 1 is a hymn, however, we would do well to hesitate to put too much stress on the definition of a single word, without testing it by the witness of scripture as a whole. For the purpose of singing the hymn, it may be sufficient simply to note that God gives humans a role—a privileged role—to play within creation. The nature and content of that privilege will need to be developed by examining all of scripture.

Fourth, the various aspects of creation call forth a particular attitude on the part of the singers: a sense of wonder. As each of the days is presented with its powerful creations and the goodness of those creations, the singers are implicitly invited to delight in the intricacy of the stars in the heavens, and in plants and animals bursting forth with life.

Possibly it is not reading too much anthropomorphism into the text to note that even God is presented as taking delight in creation. When Genesis 1 says that God saw the light or the life of the plants and animals to be good, it may not merely be indicating the goodness of these things, but also God's *enjoyment* of the goodness of these things. If so, God's delight reinforces the singers' sense of awe: "If God finds such joy in the intricacies of creation, then we will, too. And with great and overflowing wonder will our hearts offer yet more praise to the One who made all this splendor."

These four themes are not developed in full detail within the Genesis 1 hymn, but hymns work by moving our hearts, rather than by developing details. Just as the opening hymn of a service of worship unites our voices in praise to God, the Bible begins with a hymn intended to move our hearts to devotion and faithfulness, as it recounts these four themes in poetic form: creation is good; God is sovereign over all creation; humans have a special role within creation; and the goodness of creation and the sovereignty of the Creator call us to wonder and worship.

Summary

As readers, we learn to recognize different uses of language, such as the difference between a comic strip and a news report, or between a song text and a scientific textbook. In the same way, we can learn to recognize the different kinds of literature in scripture.

A close reading of Genesis 1 gives us many hints that we should not understand it as a historical report but rather as a hymn of praise to God. It uses poetic features, such as repetition and parallelism, to move us to wonder and worship. It reminds us of divine truths: God has created all things good; God is sovereign; God gives humans a role to play within creation; and God calls us to lives of gratitude.

Study Questions

1. How is a comic strip different from a news report, or a song text from a scientific textbook? What are some of the characteristics of these different types of literature?
2. What hints does the Bible give us that Genesis 1 is not a historical report?
3. What are some of the characteristics of Hebrew poetry that Genesis 1 employs?
4. Is Genesis 1 true? What kinds of truths is it trying to convey?
5. What does Genesis 1 tell us about God's character? What does it tell us about the purpose of our lives?
6. Why might the Bible include this hymn of praise at its very beginning?

PART II

GENES, ENVIRONMENT, HISTORY:
WHAT REALLY DETERMINES US?

Chapter 4

Do Genes Control Us?

R. David Cole

Developments in Genetic Research

Almost weekly we learn of genetic factors that account for physical traits such as eye color or blood type, diseases such as diabetes or Alzheimer's, and behavior patterns such as homosexuality or violence.[1] The Human Genome Project has greatly stimulated work in this area. This fifteen-year research program will reveal the chemical structure, positions, and functions of the 50,000 to 100,000 **genes*** in the human **genome** (that is, the entire set of genes that each generation inherits from its predecessors).[2]

This knowledge has great benefit. The discovery of faulty genes could explain a disease from which a person is suffering. Doctors might be able to identify an incipient disease and begin treatment to restrain its onslaught. Scientists might be able to develop gene therapies (that is, the implantation of healthy functional genes into patients whose genes are faulty), as well as new drugs.

Yet this knowledge also poses dangers. Knowledge of an individual's genetic profile might constitute an invasion of privacy. Employers and insurance companies might discriminate against individuals

---

*For further explanation of terms that are in boldface where they first appear, see the glossary at the end of this chapter

whose genetic profile reveals a tendency toward a certain disease or an undesirable trait.

The ability to alter genes also raises difficult questions. Which interventions provide sufficient benefits to justify the costs? Who pays these costs, and who is allowed to benefit from this technology? Moreover, disturbing efforts to redesign humans (eugenics) might appear.

The issue that sets the context for the present chapter is the effect of this new genetic research on our view of human nature and moral responsibility. On the one hand, biologists over the past half-century have increasingly defined humans structurally and functionally in terms of physics and chemistry. It is now clear that much of what makes us who we are biologically comes from our parents in chemical form (sperm and ovum).

On the other hand, explanations of life as chemical structures and chemical processes revive an old question in a new form: Are humans completely predetermined by their genes? How much do genes determine human potentials and limitations? To what extent can genetic determinations be transcended?[3]

Design Information Passes between Generations as Genes in Chromosomes

It only takes a glance around the supper table at a family reunion to recognize that everyone looks much like everyone else. Yet no two are identical (with the rare exception of identical twins). Moreover, "blood" relatives resemble each other more than the in-laws. Why has the basic design of the human being remained the same? And why do certain inherited characteristics stubbornly maintain themselves throughout the generations, even as much variation occurs?

The inheritance of both similarities and differences can be understood in molecular terms. Mother and father coauthor an instruction book that is passed to their child and guides his or her development. This instruction book, in the form of **DNA (deoxyribonucleic acid)** molecules, contains design information for thousands upon thousands of chemical structures.

The design for each structure is called its gene, and the instructions in each gene are spelled out in DNA as a chain of hundreds of chemical subunits called **nucleotides**. These nucleotides are arranged in a particular sequence, just as a printed instruction book for one's car or refrigerator carries messages by arranging the twenty-six letters of the English alphabet. In the gene, there are four letters, the four nucleotides abbreviated **A, T, C,** and **G**. The father and the mother contribute nearly matching sets of genetic instructions to their child. The father's set is the DNA that the sperm injects into the ovum during fertilization; the mother's set is the ovum's DNA.

In both the sperm and the egg, the genes are contained in twenty-three particles called **chromosomes.** Each chromosome consists of one piece of DNA. It strings together an enormous number of genes, each of which is composed of many A, T, C, and G subunits. The genes in all other human cells (not sperm and egg) are contained in forty-six chromosomes. In both males and females, forty-four of these forty-six chromosomes occur as pairs of **homologous chromosomes**. The other two chromosomes, sometimes called the **sex chromosomes**, are either a homologous pair, designated X chromosomes (in the female), or a heterologous pair, that is, an X chromosome and a Y chromosome (in the male).

The laws of inheritance determine that each pair of a child's chromosomes consists of one chromosome from each parent. Although the chromosomes of each homologous pair are very much alike, they are not identical. In earlier generations, minor variations (**mutations**) occasionally occurred in the fine structure of the DNA. Since the parents do not have a common genealogy, their DNA differs to some extent.

Each version, or variant, is known as an **allele** of the gene. If the two alleles of a gene are identical in the homologous pair, then the person is termed homozygous; if the alleles differ, the person is heterozygous. In the case of homologous chromosomes, an allele with normal function in one can usually compensate for a deficient allele in the other. In the case of a heterologous pair of chromosomes (in the male sex chromosomes), no compensation is possible; most of the genes of the X chromosome are missing from the Y.

Structural Differences in DNA Are the Source of Genetic Variations*

Because a child inherits only half of its father's genes and half of its mother's, the genetic cards are shuffled between generations. This shuffling, however, does not fully account for the variation in the inherited characteristics (that is, **phenotypes**) of family members; other factors are also at work. Mutations can occur in nucleotide sequences of DNA, as when DNA is damaged by various forms of radiation, or when errors occur during DNA synthesis.

In most cases, a mutation is inconsequential. It affects a single cell out of many. But when the mutation occurs in a sperm or ovum, it may be passed to offspring and amplified as the DNA is replicated (see **replication**) and the offspring grows and develops.

An especially important source of mutation arises during the formation of sperm and eggs. Although most of a mother's cells have twenty-three pairs of chromosomes, twenty-three from each of her parents, the mother's ova are each constructed with twenty-three unpaired chromosomes. An early step in the construction of an unpaired chromosome is a special process (**meiosis**) that exchanges homologous sections between the mother's corresponding paired chromosomes. Each (unpaired) chromosome in an ovum is therefore a hybrid of a pair of chromosomes inherited by the mother (from her parents). Similarly, each sperm chromosome is a hybrid of a corresponding pair of paternal chromosomes. The exchanges of chromosomal sections during meiosis cause breaks in the DNA, and errors in rejoining the DNA strands (mutations) occasionally result.

A famous case illustrating the significance of mutation in the heterologous pair of (sex) chromosomes was the appearance of hemophilia in Queen Victoria's family. A mutation occurred spontaneously in a gene that produced a **protein** necessary for the primary blood

---

*This section and the next three (pp. 56–62) answer questions that particularly interested readers might have about the construction of dynamic feedback networks. These sections also suggest the biologist's awe at the intricate beauty and power of these networks.

Some readers, however, may wish to skim through this material. It is not necessary to understand completely the scientific explanations given in these four sections in order to grasp the significance of the rest of the chapter.

clotting process. The mutant gene produced an ineffective protein, with the result that even minor wounds sometimes resulted in death before slow, secondary processes could staunch the blood flow. No women in the Queen's family had difficulty with blood clotting, but some of the men did, most famously the crown prince of Russia.

The gene for the clotting factor was in the X chromosome. Some of the women (those with homozygous genes for clotting) carried two fully functional genes in their pair of X chromosomes, and others (heterozygous) carried a functional gene on one X chromosome and a faulty gene on the other. All the women were able to clot blood because they possessed at least one good gene. Those men who carried a good gene in their single X chromosome clotted blood effectively, but any who inherited a faulty gene in their only X chromosome were hemophiliacs.

Design Information Is Transmitted to All Cells in Developmental Growth

The fertilized ovum, a single cell, divides into two cells. Each of these cells then divides, and the total number of cells becomes four. Cell doubling continues as the embryo grows into a fetus, a child, and finally an adult with its billions of cells. Because all the cells of an individual (except for sperm and eggs) have identical sets of genes, each cell division requires duplication of the genes.

A look at the structure of DNA reveals how genetic information is replicated, so that every progeny cell receives a complete set of genes. Each of the A, T, C, and G nucleotide subunits of DNA consists of a **base** linked to a sugar, which in turn is linked to a phosphate. In a polynucleotide (a chain of nucleotides), phosphates form bridges between the sugars of the nucleotides, leaving the bases to dangle from the chain of alternating phosphates and sugars.

The DNA molecule has two polynucleotide chains twisted around each other to form a "double helix" (see upper part of Figure 1).* Each polynucleotide strand is a strong chain of alternating sugars and phosphates, with a base attached to each sugar. Each base,

---

*Figures appear on p. 70

besides being strongly bound to a sugar on its own strand, is more weakly bound to a base on the other strand.

The **base pairs** facing each other are always either A and T, or C and G; no other combinations fit together. The two strands of DNA are thus complementary to one another (see **complementarity**), and the sequence of bases on one strand can be deduced from the sequence on the other. The inside of the double helix formed by the two intertwined nucleotide strands could be likened to a spiral staircase where each step is a pair of complementary bases. This complementary base-pairing of nucleotide strands provides the basis not only for replicating DNA, but also for passing messages between generations and for applying DNA information to the synthesis of proteins.

Shortly before cell division, the DNA is duplicated. The two strands of DNA separate, and each strand is used as a template (pattern) for the synthesis of a new complementary strand. Individual, complementary mononucleotides are lined up opposite the exposed bases of the template, and the mononucleotides are stitched together by a molecular machine (called DNA polymerase) to form a new polynucleotide strand (see lower part of Figure 1 at the end of the chapter). Two double helices result, each identical to the original, one for each of the progeny. Each progeny cell receives one original polynucleotide strand and a complementary new strand.

Genetic Information Is Expressed in Protein Synthesis

Most of the time, the cell is not occupied with division, but with the ongoing business of living. That business requires the cooperative action of 50,000 to 100,000 components, mostly the kind of molecules called "proteins." Genes design protein structures, and proteins do the body's work and create phenotypes.

A protein is a chain of hundreds of subunits called **amino acids**. A messenger is needed to carry the coded instructions from the nucleus of the cell, where the DNA is confined, to outside the nucleus, where the **ribosome** (the protein synthesizing machinery) is located. This messenger is a molecule called **messenger RNA** (mRNA). **RNA** (**ribonucleic acid**), like DNA, is a chain of nucleotides. But its sugar component is slightly modified, and it is a single strand rather than a double strand. RNA, like DNA, has four nucleotide bases, but it uses U in place of the T of DNA.

Genomic information is passed from DNA to RNA by the synthesis of a polynucleotide chain whose bases are complementary to the bases in one of the DNA strands (Figure 2). The mRNA is released from the DNA template and exits the nucleus to take part in a multistep chemical process that forms a polymeric chain of amino acids. Each amino acid is encoded in DNA as a particular sequence of three nucleotides; for example, TTC in DNA is transcribed (see **transcription**) as AAG in mRNA, and the latter is then translated (see **translation**) into the amino acid lysine (Figure 2). DNA thus contains a recipe for each protein.

The primary structure of an average protein is a chain of about three hundred amino acids of twenty kinds. The amino acids are lined up in a particular sequence, which differs from one protein to the next. Since amino acids differ in chemical character, each kind of protein also differs. To accomplish the complicated work of the human body, tens of thousands of proteins are needed. Each has a highly specific function, most frequently promoting a single kind of chemical reaction. In specifying an amino acid sequence, the information in the gene must also cause the string of connected amino acids to fold itself into a three-dimensional structure unique to the particular kind of protein that has that function.

Most proteins are designed to coordinate their functions with those of other proteins. Integration of the functions of many proteins into large networks indirectly links large numbers of chemical processes. These webs of chemical processes are frequently "feedback" systems that allow an organism to shift its balance of activities according to changes in the demand for the system's output. In short, such networks allow the organism to adapt to environmental change. The sensitivity of each protein to other proteins or to small chemicals requires that the design in the genes not only specify the primary function of the protein and its correct folding but also respond to these chemical "feed-back" signals.

Despite all these strictures on amino acid sequences, proteins can tolerate some mutations. The degree of tolerance differs from one part of the protein structure to another. Mutations might be lethal, might partially inactivate the protein, or might have no substantial effect. Occasionally a mutation creates a new kind of function.

A single gene rarely accounts for a particular phenotype. It is estimated, for example, that less than two percent of genetic diseases are caused by single gene deficiencies.[4] Even when a particular (faulty) gene can be identified with a certain disease, its role can be complex.[5] An example of a monogenic disease is cystic fibrosis, where a defect in one particular gene is sufficient to cause the disease.[6] The more common situation is represented by cancer, where mutations in one gene seem necessary for some kinds of cancer but are insufficient to cause the disease unless other genes are also damaged.[7] Normal characteristics—such as body measurements, intelligence, and cholesterol metabolism—also depend on the interactions of many different genes. This multigenic dependence is reflected in the fact that most biological characteristics exhibit a wide range of variation—for example, the heights of humans.

Cell Specialization Requires Regulation of Gene Expression

The cell's DNA contains more than the nucleotide sequences that code for amino acid sequences. The major portion of DNA is noncoding. (In addition, a small fraction of the DNA encodes RNA structures that are not translated to proteins.)

While we do not understand all the functions of this non-coding DNA, part of it is used in the control of **gene expression**, as has been amply demonstrated in such simple organisms as bacteria. Each gene carries "regulatory" sequences. In interaction with regulatory molecules, frequently proteins, these regulatory sequences turn gene expression on or off, or adjust the rate of transcription into mRNA. These interactions play a role in networks of feedback control.

The regulation of genes in the human body, as in all animal bodies, is vastly more complicated than in the single-celled bacterium. The human body has many specialized tissues and organs, each of which has several cell types. Each cell type implements only a small subset of its genes. It regulates the extent of gene expression to produce the right amounts of proteins. Most of the genes are repressed (see **gene repression**).

The functional needs of the cell, tissue, or organ determine which of the many possible combinations of genes will be expressed. Genes restrict cell function to a limited range of possibilities, but they cannot determine which possibility will actually occur. The cell's context determines the extent to which the gene is able to put its instructions into effect.

The development of human cell types and tissues is characterized by a process called differentiation. The mechanisms that produce differentiation are not well understood. In plants, differentiation can frequently be reversed, and development begun anew. Thus, a complete, differentiated rose bush can grow from the stem of a rose. Generally, animals are incapable of such feats. The limited dedifferentiation that occurs in cancer formation leads to localized, abnormal growth. To restart a normal program of development, highly differentiated animals synthesize fresh, single strands of DNA (in sperm and ovum, respectively) and combine them in the single cell of the ovum, thus circumventing the need for reversal of differentiation before a new program of differentiation begins.

We are not entirely sure why differentiation cannot normally be reversed in animals. One possible explanation is that DNA undergoes structural modification in the process of differentiation, with the result that the repression of genes in differentiated cells cannot be reversed. Another possible explanation is that protein matrices entrap the DNA, acting somewhat like a crab trap in preventing dedifferentiation. A long succession of precisely timed steps during embryonic and fetal development would build up a matrix of DNA and many interacting proteins. To extract proteins from the matrix in correct order and, then, to retrace the long sequence of steps necessary for development and differentiation would require a precisely timed program that appears not to occur naturally.

The recent cloning of a lamb from adult DNA will probably help to answer questions about the mechanisms that underlie differentiation. In mature, organized tissues, differentiated cells do not divide. In this case, however, scientists induced mammary cells from an adult sheep to go through a number of cell divisions by dispersing them in nutrient-containing dishes. After several rounds of division, the cells were starved just enough to stop their dividing. One such cell was fused with an ovum cell whose DNA had been sucked out through a needle. The resulting fused cell thus contained the DNA from the adult mammary tissue, the cell contents of the mammary cell, and the non-DNA contents of the ovum.

After a short resting period, this composite cell was implanted into the uterus of a surrogate sheep to develop into a lamb whose DNA was identical to that of the donor of the original mammary tissue. The mammary DNA had been stripped of all repressing structures and was able to start differentiation all over again, guided by non-DNA factors of the ovum into which it had been introduced. Where in this procedure the donor's DNA was derepressed, and how, are not clear. What is clear is that under special circumstances the DNA of differentiated tissue can escape the control of the tissue's context. Conversely, this experiment shows the power that context exerts in the control of gene expression.

Adaptation of Organisms Shows Environmental Control over Genes

To survive in a dynamic world, organisms and cells must be designed to adapt to a wide range of environmental conditions. Adaptation in humans is reflected in the body's response to altitude change and strenuous exercise, but less conspicuous adaptation occurs continuously. While some of these changes are metabolic and do not require changes in gene expression, others require repression of some genes and activation of others.

A gene is repressed neither by destroying it nor by changing its base sequence, but by blocking the transcription of its nucleotide code, the first step in the synthesis of the corresponding protein. The mechanisms for gene repression and activation are sensitive to physical and chemical forces inside and outside the cell. Some newly induced patterns of gene expression can be reversed by a return to initial conditions, but in animal cells some adaptive changes are irreversible. The environment to which an organism adapts thus controls which genes can actualize their potentials, and which cannot. The genes, of course, define which adaptations can be actualized in the first place.

Emotions Exert Control over Gene Expression through Hormones

The dynamics of adaptation in higher animals are illustrated by hormones. Hormones are secreted from cells in one part of the body for transport to target cells elsewhere. When the hormones bind to the target cells, they change the structure of receptor proteins on the surface of the cells, which triggers a series of functional changes within the cells, inducing the organism to adapt to changes in circumstances.

Parts of the hormonal system respond to changes in mental state. Stress, for example, induces the secretion of adrenaline and glucocorticosteroids, which increase blood flow, redistribute the blood, and cause other physiological changes, many of which can be construed as preparing a person for physical battle or flight.

The sequence of bases in the genome specifies the ways a person can respond to these signals and adapt to changing circumstances. But it is also clear that the base sequence is not a sufficient explanation. The genome predetermines potential states of being and behavior, but it does not predetermine a person to any one particular state.

Learning and Choice Can Modulate Gene Expression

One of the most active fronts in biological research today is concerned with the operations of the brain in processing sensory information and in using language, solving problems, and learning.[8] A focus on learning is especially useful here. Current observations and postulates suggest analogies between learning and long-term cell adaptation. These analogies allow a role for non-genetic factors (such as choice), along with DNA, in the development of our personhood.

A major kind of cell in the brain is the **neuron**, which possesses numerous long, thin extensions called **dendrites**, and a thicker extension termed the **axon**. Every neuron makes contact with others by its dendrites, thereby constructing a vast network of interconnected cells. When a neuron receives a signal from a dendrite, it transmits the signal through its axon to the dendrites of one or more other neurons. The point at which nerve impulses pass between neurons is called a **synapse**. Memory and learning are characterized by functional and morphological changes in the networks of synapses. The neuronal networks with their many trillions of synapses constitute the "hard wiring" of brain circuitry.[9]

While genes predetermine the potential designs for these circuits, as they do for all structures of the body, it appears that learning causes new synapses to develop among the existing ones.[10] Experiments with mice have shown that new, complex, neural circuits are added as brain development continues.[11] Furthermore, rodents reared in complex and stimulating conditions have more synapses and dendrites than animals raised in simpler circumstances. Related experiments reveal that synaptic networks are built up by all kinds of mental activity and that learning builds up the network in adults as well as in children. For this reason, learning and other mental exercise help to prevent the decline of mental capacities that often accompany aging.

Consistent with the notion that these structural changes represent adaptation is the fact that they are essentially irreversible. Mechanisms for structural changes in long-term memory apparently alter the pattern of gene expression and modulate protein synthesis.[12] Neural processes such as learning and choosing thus add specifications to the formation of our intellectual apparatus beyond those set by our genes, though within the range predetermined by them.

Already constricted by genes, the scope for the exercise of will is further narrowed by environmental factors. The notion of learning as mental adaptation makes especially clear the connection between gene-based molecular systems and the physical and social environment. The social environment affects humans directly through the mind as well as indirectly by determining many aspects of our physical environment. Moreover, when seen as mental adaptation, learning incorporates human history into the structure and function of the brain. Constrained by all these factors, what freedom is left for the will?

Some argue that a full molecular description of the brain in interaction with the environment will provide a complete explanation of the life of the mind; "free choice" is nothing but an illusion. In this view, choice is fully determined by genes and environment. Others would agree that brain mechanisms necessarily depend on molecular processes but would dispute that those processes are a sufficient explanation of the mind.

A crucial part of this question concerns the location of initial causes. Although much research is still needed to complete the picture, it is likely that any thought can be described as a matrix of molecular causes and effects. How a thought begins, however, is another matter. It would be analogous to our having a complete description of the mechanisms of a running automobile, but no knowledge of how the motor had been activated.

Some deny the subjective experience of freedom. They conclude that the environment is sufficient to start the gene-based motor. Denial, however, does not disprove the reality of the subjective experience, nor does the vulnerability of subjective experience to illusion. Most people find the subjective experience of free choice so compelling that they believe in its reality even without an explanation of it. Even if a molecular description of brain dynamics were complete, it might still fail to give a complete explanation of how human choice originates. Resolution of the centuries-old debate over the reality of free will seems no closer now than it ever has.

Personal Responsibility in Gene Control

It is humbling to recognize how much our genome determines who we are. It sets rigid boundaries on what we can do and be. Those of us who want to be great athletes can control our weight by diet or build our muscles by exercise or even with hormones, but our genome sets limits. We cannot shape our bodies just anyway we please. Some of us would like to have great intellects. We can teach and train our brains up to a point, but some minds evidently have more potential than others.

Nevertheless, these two examples show that personal choice is effective to a degree and that we hold some responsibility for choosing well. Most genes merely "predispose" us to biological characteristics, such as athletic ability, intelligence, or violent behavior. How these characteristics come to be expressed depends on complex interactions among genetic and non-genetic factors.

As in the parable of the talents, our genome and our environmental history endow us with greater or lesser potential, and it is our responsibility to optimize our lives within these boundaries. In choosing to maintain our bodies in good shape, or to develop our intellects, we partially control the genome. Even with the strongest motives and discipline, however, the degree of success will differ from one person to the next. Because most biological traits (especially behaviors) are multigenic and multifactorial, they will be expressed among people in continuous gradation over a wide range. Despite any genes that may help to account for obesity or violence, most of us can choose to curb our appetite or hold our temper, but it is harder for some of us than for others—and perhaps for a very few it is even impossible. With this picture in mind, courts of law will be challenged to determine how to assign degrees of responsibility for aberrant behaviors, which depend on genes, environment, history, and presumably free will.

For those of us who believe in free will and the responsibility that accompanies it, it is intriguing to consider how free will can interact with genetic systems to maximize the realization of some potentialities and to minimize others. Synergy between the human mind and the patterns of gene expression in the brain could be a model for a broader concept of the human. The pattern of gene expression in the brain and body can be regarded as the substrate on which the human spirit continually acts, modifying the substrate for subsequent interactions. Rather than argue about the relative importance of body and spirit in the determination of the human, we might do better to recognize this creative synergy. We are formed from the interplay of our genes and the history of our circumstances, along with the motivations of our spirit. No matter how great the magnitude of genetic determinism, it need not overwhelm our sense of responsibility for who we are and what we become. The fact that our personal history is incorporated into the very fabric of our brains challenges us to discipline our lives in ways that honor and serve our Lord.

NOTES

1. Leon Jaroff, "Keys to the Kingdom," *Time-Special Issue* 148, no. 14 (Fall 1996): 24; and Philip Elmer-Dewitt, "The Genetics Revolution," *Time* 143 (January 17, 1994): 46.

2. U.S. Departments of Energy and of Health and Human Services, "Understanding Our Genetic Inheritance. The Human Genome Project:

The First Five Years, FY 1991–1995," N.I.H. Publication No. 90-1590 (April 1990); and Francis Collins and David Galas, "A New Five-Year Plan for the U.S. Human Genome Project," *Science* 262 (October 1, 1993): 43.

3. Most of the biology presented in this chapter is commonly found in college-level text books on general biology or molecular biology. See, for example: N. A. Campbell, L. G. Mitchell, and J. B. Reece, *Biology: Concepts and Connections* (Menlo Park, Calif.: Benjamin Cummings, 1994).

4. Richard C. Strohman, "Ancient Genomes, Wise Bodies, Unhealthy People: Limits of a Genetic Paradigm in Biology and Medicine," *University of California/Health Net Lecture Series* (October 12, 1992).

5. Neil Risch and Kathleen Merikangas, "The Future of Genetic Studies of Complex Human Diseases," *Science* 273 (September 13, 1996): 1516.

6. Francis S. Collins, "Cystic Fibrosis: Molecular Biology and Therapeutic Implications," *Science* 256 (May 8, 1992): 774.

7. Rachel Nowak, "Breast Cancer Gene Offers Surprises," *Science* 265 (September 23, 1994): 1796; and Jean Marx, "A Second Breast Cancer Susceptibility Gene is Found," *Science* 271 (January 5, 1996): 30.

8. Ronald Kotulak, *Inside the Brain* (Kansas City: Andrews & McMeel, 1996).

9. Eric R. Kandel and Thomas J. O'Dell, "Are Adult Learning Mechanisms Also Used for Development?" *Science* 258 (October 9, 1992): 243.

10. See Kotulak.

11. See Kandel and O'Dell, 243.

12. Morgan Sheng and Michael E. Greenberg, "The Regulation and Function of Cfos and Other Intermediate Early Genes in the Nervous System," *Neuron* 4 (April 1990): 477.

Glossary

A: Abbreviation for adenine, one of the bases in DNA and RNA; it pairs with T or U.

Allele: The form of a gene that is inherited separately from each parent. In most chromosomes, therefore, there are two.

Amino acid: The subunits that are linked together in a chain to form a protein. There are twenty kinds of amino acids, differing widely in chemical character.

Axon: The thick extension from the body of a neuron (nerve cell).

Base: The part of a nucleotide that is attached to the sugar. In DNA, it is adenine, thymine, guanine, or cytosine. In RNA, it is adenine, uracil, guanine, or cytosine.

Base pair: Two bases held together by weak bonds. The two strands of the DNA helix are held together by the bonding of many base pairs.

Chromosome: The structure that contains a single piece of double-stranded DNA, linking many genes.

Complementarity: This refers to the mutual binding of matching bases: A with T, C with G, and A with U.

C: Abbreviation for cytosine, one of the bases in DNA and RNA; it pairs with G.

Dendrite: A long, thin extension from the surface of a neuron (nerve cell).

Deoxyribonucleic acid: Formed by two strands of nucleotides twisted together to form a helix (double helix). The strands are held together by complementary base pairing.

DNA: See Deoxyribonucleic acid.

Gene: The fundamental unit of inheritance, usually defined by its biological function, although it can also be identified by its chemical structure.

Gene expression: The conversion of the gene's coded information into a gene-product, which is usually a protein.

Gene repression: A process that prevents the expression of a gene.

Genome: All the genetic material in the chromosomes of an organism.

G: Abbreviation for guanine, one of the bases in DNA and RNA; it pairs with C.

Homologous chromosomes: A pair of chromosomes with the same genes (defined functionally) in the same linear order.

Meiosis: A process in the production of sperm and ova. Single, rather than paired, chromosomes are passed to the sperm cell or ovum.

Messenger RNA (mRNA): RNA that has a base sequence complementary to that of a gene. It is the template for protein synthesis.

Mutation: A change in the base sequence of DNA, or in the amino acid sequence of a protein.

Nucleotide: The subunit of DNA or RNA that consists of a base connected to a sugar (deoxyribose in DNA, or ribose in RNA), to which a phosphate is attached.

Neuron: The type of nerve cell that transmits signals as electrical impulses.

Phenotype: An observable characteristic of an organism.

Protein: A large molecular structure. It is made with a chain of linked amino acids folded to a precise, three-dimensional shape. Some proteins are complexes formed from multiple, folded chains. There are tens of thousands of kinds of proteins, each with a unique function.

Replication: The process of synthesizing a new, complementary strand on an old strand of deoxyribonucleotides to make double-stranded DNA.

Ribonucleic Acid: A chain-like molecule with nucleotide subunits. Each nucleotide is one of four bases (A, U, C, or G) linked to a ribose (sugar), which in turn is linked to a phosphate.

Ribosome: Made of proteins and RNA, it is the cell's machine that synthesizes proteins using messenger RNA as a template.

RNA: See Ribonucleic acid.

Sex chromosome: The X or Y chromosome in humans. Females have a pair of homologous X chromosomes; males have one X and one Y.

Synapse: The juncture at which signals pass from a dendrite of an axon of one neuron to a dendrite on another neuron.

T: Abbreviation for thymine, a base found in DNA; it pairs with A.

Transcription: The synthesis of a strand of messenger RNA from a single strand template of DNA. The base sequence of the messenger RNA is complementary to that of the template.

Translation: The process of synthesizing a chain of amino acids with a sequence corresponding to the nucleotide sequence in a messenger RNA. Translation is the principal feature of protein synthesis.

U: Abbreviation for uracil, a base found in RNA; it pairs with A.

Figure 1

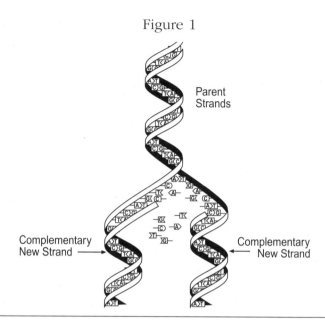

Parent Strands

Complementary New Strand →

← Complementary New Strand

Figure 2

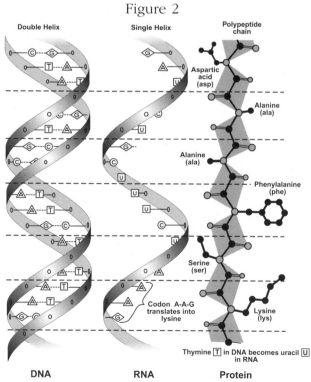

Double Helix

Single Helix

Polypeptide chain

Aspartic acid (asp)

Alanine (ala)

Alanine (ala)

Phenylalanine (phe)

Serine (ser)

Codon A-A-G translates into lysine

Lysine (lys)

Thymine T in DNA becomes uracil U in RNA

DNA

RNA

Protein

Summary

The Human Genome Project is in the process of locating genes in human chromosomes and determining their chemical structure. Brief reports in the popular media may give us the impression that each gene inevitably expresses itself as a particular trait or disease. In reality, genes interact in complex ways among each other and with the environment and human choices to define ultimately who we are and what we do.

Genes encode the design information for all the different parts and processes of the body. Each of the human's 50,000–100,000 genes contains the design information for a single chemical structure. Nearly all human traits depend on the interaction of many different genes. Moreover, the molecular processes directed by genes adapt to their environment through elaborate feedback systems that increase or decrease the activity of these processes according to the body's needs. Physical, emotional, or psychological factors affect which genes express themselves, and how, as the brain regulates hormones and other chemical signals.

Because much adaption is irreversible, it becomes part of an organism's history. In addition, neural activities such as learning and choosing modify the gene-based "hard wiring" of the brain, resulting in what might be called "mental adaptation." Thus, while genes rigidly set our potentials and limitations, history and choice also influence the actual outcome. In a profound sense, we are free, though always within a range of possibilities set by our genes and environment.

Study Questions

1. It is possible that genetic research will establish a link between aberrant behaviors—such as violence, alcoholism, and sexual offenses—and particular mutant genes. What problems will judges and juries have in determining guilt? What role could the church play in helping society to resolve these questions?
2. If a gene analysis revealed that your child had a gene predisposing him or her to violence, obesity, or drug addiction, how would it affect your plans for raising him or her? How far would you go in trying to control your child's behaviors?

3. If at the age of eighteen you discovered that you have a gene predisposing you to melanoma (sunlight-induced skin cancer), how would you change your lifestyle? What would you do if you had a gene predisposing you to violence or alcoholism?

4. How can social factors affect the kind of physical environment in which children will grow up? How can they affect a child's ability to learn? What is more important in determining a child's future: these social and psychological factors, or his or her genes?

5. If human traits and behaviors are the result of complex interactions among genes, environment, history, and choice, how does the church best minister to individuals? How would we best design programs and ministries for children, adults, elderly people, addicts, prisoners, educators, physicians, or lawyers?

Chapter 5

Perspectives on the Origins and Evolution of Humanity: In Whose Image Are We Really Made?

I. Lehr Brisbin, Jr.

The Diversity of Life: Evolution and Classification

The "green" environmental revolution has taught us that we humans are an integral part of the environmental/ecological systems that we share with other creatures. Whether they include skyscrapers and city parks, suburban lawns, tropical rain forests, or arctic tundra, these environmental systems impinge upon and interact with human cultures. For humans, as for other living organisms, these environmental contexts help to determine which of the individuals produced in a given generation will be best suited to survive and will produce offspring.

Over the past century, research has confirmed and scientists have more fully studied this process of natural selection and organic evolution, originally described by Charles Darwin. It is this process that has produced our own human species and the rich variety of living things that surround us, in response to environmental and cultural changes over both geologic and historical time.

A visit to a modern zoo quickly reveals the vastly different degrees to which other life forms of this planet resemble humans: from a high degree of dissimilarity between ourselves and smaller organisms (such as sponges, insects, and other animals without backbones) to a high degree of similarity, which even a casual observer notes between the appearances, facial expressions, and social behaviors of the higher primates, particularly the great apes, and humans.

The varying degrees of similarity between living organisms are the basis of taxonomy, the field of science that seeks to categorize living creatures according to their degree of relationship. In descending order of complexity, these taxonomic classifications include the kingdom, phylum, order, class, family, genus, species, and subspecies.

These classifications were initially made on the basis of structure and appearance, including both external and internal anatomy. They were particularly based on structures such as bones, skulls, and teeth that tend to persist in the fossil record. More recently, scientists have added quantitative analyses of behavioral traits and particularly molecular genetic profiles based on DNA analyses to their arsenal of criteria for determining taxonomic affinities and past evolutionary/ancestral relationships.

As the areas of behavioral and particularly molecular genetic taxonomy have come of age, it has been remarkable to note the degree to which their findings agree with, and even confirm, earlier findings based on anatomical structures. This agreement includes taxonomic categories. Animal species whose skulls and skeletal characteristics are more similar to one another tend to have more similar patterns of DNA base-pair sequences.

What is even more remarkable are the relatively close estimates of the time that has passed since major groups or species or organisms have diverged from one another in the evolutionary process. Paleontologists determine these time periods by such techniques as radiocarbon or potassium-argon isotope dating of fossil material and/or comparable knowledge concerning the ages and rates of accumulation of various layers in the geologic strata in which the fossils are found.

Molecular genetic analyses of the timing of evolutionary events utilize a very different approach. Based on intricate knowledge of the stability of the DNA molecule, scientists can estimate the rate at which normal mutational events (for example, bombardment by the background radiation of cosmic rays from outer space) would be expected to break certain chemical bonds within the DNA molecule. They can estimate the amount of time required for the gradual accumulation of more and more mutational base-pair sequence rearrangements.[1]

It is comforting to note the degree to which this "molecular clock" approach to the timing of evolutionary events agrees with the timing predicted by the paleontological record. This agreement provides cogent support for both the correctness of the taxonomic affinities that have been proposed and for the objective reality of the evolutionary process itself.[2]

Nowhere have these processes of evolutionary descent and taxonomic relatedness been subjected to more detailed examination, discussion, and verification than in the case of the relationship between the human species and the living great apes. Pioneered by the late Dr. Louis B. Leakey, Dr. Donald Johanson, and their colleagues, this research has drawn on the fossil record of our earlier human ancestors (particularly those from the now notorious region of paleontological excavation and research in Kenya, Tanzania, and Ethiopia) to advance our understanding of our early ancestors and their evolutionary development towards the species *Homo sapiens.*[3]

Here again, advances in the area of DNA analyses and the application of the "molecular clock," and the findings of past generations of paleontologists, are coming together in important and revealing ways. State-of-the-art genetic analyses based on the polymerase chain reaction (PCR) are capable of reproducing thousands or even millions of copies from the smallest quantities of DNA. Scientists are now able to recover and analyze the structure of small fragments of ancient DNA from fossil material that is hundreds or in some cases even thousands of years old![4]

Our Place in the Scheme of Things

Whether based on fossil evidence and paleontology, molecular genetics, or plain old-fashioned commonsense observation, there is little doubt or disagreement as to where to classify our human species in the major groups of the animal kingdom. The bony column encasing our spinal cord clearly classifies us as a vertebrate; our (usually evident) hair and production of milk to nurse our young further place us in the class Mammalia. Within the mammals, moreover, it is obvious that our closest affinities are not with platypuses, kangaroos, dogs, horses, pigs, whales, or mice, but rather with the apes and monkeys of the order Primates. It is equally obvious that our affinities are more with the great apes than with the lower primates such as lemurs, marmosets, and monkeys.

From there on, however, things get a bit sticky. When we consider our taxonomic relationship to such species as gorillas and chimpanzees, we may experience discomfort, especially if we believe the human species to be "made in the image of God" and therefore completely and categorically different from all other species of animals on the face of the earth.

Certainly on the basis of external appearance, internal anatomy, and even behavior and emotion, apes such as the chimpanzee are *not* completely and categorically different from humans. In some important ways, particularly in the area of behavior and intelligence, a number of the great apes and humans are clearly much more like each other than any other living creature on earth. Abundant data from molecular genetics further confirm the close relationship between humans and chimpanzees—98 percent of the DNA base-pair sequences of humans and chimps are homologous.[5] If we would affirm that we, the human species, are "made in the image of God," we seem forced to conclude that chimpanzees and gorillas are "pretty much" made in the image of God too!

Setting Us Apart: The "Soul Man"

Despite these similarities, we are clearly *not* chimpanzees or any other form of modern great ape. What is it, then, that so clearly separates us (especially in our own mind) from such apes and that places our species in a category all its own? While these distinguishing features are surprisingly few in number, they are *awesome* in scope and consequence: (1) the possession of a soul or a spiritual nature, (2) the size and degree of development of the brain, particularly the cerebral cortex, and (3) the development and use of a complex spoken language.

It must be noted in passing that characteristics often associated with the presence of a soul or with a spiritual nature are also evident in a number of non-human species, particularly the higher apes.[6] The careful, well-known work of Jane Goodall on the behavior of chimpanzees in the wild clearly shows that they somehow understand the significance of death. Elephants too have been known to respond in a strikingly complex and ritualistic fashion upon encountering the tusks, bones, or other body parts of fallen comrades.[7]

Although we will never know how early man's direct non-human ancestors regarded the death of one of their kin, there is evidence that one form of our primitive ancestors, the Neanderthals, routinely buried their dead, sometimes in a careful (dare we say loving?) fashion (for example, with flowers), suggesting some form of spiritual awareness.[8] Here again, it is a matter of gradation and degree rather than an abrupt and distinctive difference that sets us apart from other living and evolving creatures.

In contrast to the matter of spirituality and the possession of a soul, the development of the brain and a complex spoken language can be addressed in a more factual and straightforward manner. Recent research suggests that these two features may be more closely related to one another than previously thought.[9] Advances in the area of DNA research are beginning to tie these two features together, while providing a context in which better to understand the fossil record of human evolutionary development and emergence as a distinct and modern species.

Out of Africa: The Long Walk to *Homo Sapiens*

As presently understood, the story of the development and emergence of our human species begins in Africa about two million years ago. While inconceivably long in relation to individual human lifetimes, family generations, and even recorded history, this history is a mere blink of an eye in geologic time. As revealed in their fossil-rich deposits, that region of the world that is now Kenya and Ethiopia was truly a "Garden of Eden." Its savannah grasslands, forest-edge habitat, benign climate, and abundant food resources and game animals were probably much like the rich African game parks of that region today. In such an area, even a fumbling/emerging prehuman with only a rudimentary ability to make and use tools and/or weapons could still obtain food and make a living, perhaps initially as much by dumb luck as by skill or cunning.[10]

On this scene appeared the first member of our genus *Homo,* a three-foot-high, tool-making anthropoid (apelike creature) with a twenty-three-ounce brain (about half the size of ours today), known as *Homo habilis.* As small as this creature's brain may have been, it was larger than that of the more primitive bipedal Australopithecenes with whom *Homo habilis* shared this prehistoric garden of plenty. Australopithecenes disappeared from the fossil record, leaving us to wonder whether the first member of our genus was also the first to succeed in out-competing or otherwise encroaching on its more dim-witted cousins.

"What goes around comes around" (something our present-day culture might do well to remember), and *Homo habilis* was in turn supplanted by a larger, more robust "brother," *Homo erectus,* who stood about six feet tall and possessed a thirty-three-ounce brain. *Homo erectus* then spread (dare we say, was driven?) out of Africa and into Europe and Asia, perhaps as a result of its growing population and/or an innate tendency to wander and disperse.

300,000 years ago, "pay-back" time came again, now for *Homo erectus,* who is clearly supplanted once and for all in the fossil record by an even bigger-brained and certainly more clever and cultured form: our own species, *Homo sapiens.*[11]

The brains of these first members of our species were not only larger (forty-five to fifty ounces), but also infinitely more complex. Generally known as the "archaic" as opposed to the "modern" type of our species, they were typified by the Neanderthals (taxonomically distinguished as the subspecies *Homo sapiens neanderthalensis*), which spread throughout Europe and southwest Asia from northeast Africa and the Middle East.

With the emergence of this most primitive member of our own species, the most important elements for the accolade "made in the image of God" had finally fallen into place. To be sure, if some of us confronted a Neanderthal personally, we might think twice before agreeing that such a creature truly had a "soul." Yet it is interesting (and discouraging!) to note that as late as the 1840s, some people in the United States were still debating whether or not Native Americans were truly human and had souls![12]

Consensus now seems to be growing that a third and final emergence of humans from eastern Africa occurred about 200,000 and perhaps as recently as 100,000 years ago, again resulting in a rapid dispersal throughout Europe and Asia. These modern-type humans had well-developed, forty-five- to fifty-ounce brains. They apparently lived side by side with the archaic-type humans, hunting the same game and using similar tools and cultural artifacts for some time before the modern types replaced the latter, who then disappeared permanently from the fossil record.[13]

This replacement/elimination of the more primitive by the more modern forms of *Homo sapiens* has been one of the most thoroughly studied and hotly debated topics in the scientific study of human origins and evolution. For one thing, we have an abundant and well-documented fossil record in comparison to the earlier stages of our human ancestry. For another, this issue has been the first testing ground for molecular genetics as a tool to advance our understanding of paleoanthropology (the study of human biology through the fossil record).

Initially, battle lines were drawn between fossil-hunting paleontologists armed with teeth and skull fragments and molecular biologists armed with laboratory-produced DNA profiles and the ticking of a molecular clock. Only recently have these two groups begun to understand and trust one another. Practitioners on each side are gradually becoming more aware of, and receptive to, what they can learn from each other.[14] As a result, we now have one of the clearest pictures yet of what it means to be a member of the human species, *Homo sapiens,* made "in the image of God."

Molecular Genetics and Mitochondrial Eve

Scientists have used three forms of molecular genetic (DNA) analysis to study the evolutionary emergence of modern-type *Homo sapiens* and their successful replacement of the contemporaneous archaic Neanderthal types: (1) analyses of mitochondrial DNA (mtDNA) to study maternal lineages of descent, leading to the so-called "mitochondrial Eve" concept, (2) studies of Y-chromosome DNA to study paternal lineages of descent, leading to the search for a DNA-defined genetic

"Adam" as a consort for our "mitochondrial Eve," and (3) studies based on unique "signatures" of nuclear DNA.[15]

While the nuclear DNA studies have been the most recent and convincing, it was the announcement in the popular press of the discovery of "mitochondrial Eve" that initially captured the public's (and church's) attention.[16] It was said that this single mother of us all was very likely black and short of stature, and that she lived somewhere in sub-Saharan Africa about 200,000 years ago.

These assertions were based on the analysis of the DNA that is found in mitochondria, small structures that are found outside the nucleus in the cell's cytoplasm. All of an individual's mitochondrial DNA comes from the mother. (Male sperm contain only nuclear DNA.) Through this mtDNA, scientists can trace maternal lines of descent without the confusion that results from the combining of different maternal and paternal sets of DNA in the nucleus during fertilization.

Extensive studies have demonstrated that the maternal lines of mtDNA—from a variety of ethnic groups throughout the world—derive from, and coalesce into, a single mtDNA type that emerged from Africa 100,000 to 200,000 years ago and then spread rapidly around the globe. Studies of the genes of the Y chromosome, which is carried only by males, and nuclear DNA genetic studies have reached similar conclusions, which are gradually coming to be reinforced and accepted by paleoanthropologists working with the fossil record.

In an elegant treatment of the issue of "mitochondrial Eve," the noted geneticist, Francisco Ayala, summarizes the diverse lines of scientific evidence on the subject, while noting that it is a misunderstanding to point to a single individual as the maternal progenitor of the entire human race. This misunderstanding has arisen from a confusion between gene genealogies and individual genealogies. As Ayala puts it,

> This Eve, however, is not the one mother from whom all humans descend, but rather a mtDNA molecule (or the woman carrier of that molecule) from which all modern mtDNA molecules descend. . . . Coalescence [of all present mtDNA types] to one ancestral gene originally present in one individual does not disallow the contemporary existence of

many other ancestors from whom we have inherited the other genes. . . . Thus, a person inherits the mtDNA from the great-grandmother in the maternal line, but also inherits other genes from the three other great-grandmothers and the four great-grandfathers (about one-eighth of the total DNA [coming] from each great-grandparent). The mtDNA that we have inherited from the mitochondrial Eve represents a four-hundred-thousandth part of the DNA present in any modern human. The rest of the DNA, 400,000 times the amount of mtDNA, was inherited from other contemporaries of the mitochondrial Eve.[17]

Ayala uses DNA profile analyses to estimate that "Eve's" contemporaries probably formed a population whose size ranged from ten thousand to more than fifty thousand reproducing individuals over the past sixty million years.

This work brings together different lines of molecular genetic study. The most important result, though it is often overlooked, is the suggestion that the members of the diverse ethnic array of our human family—from Aleut Eskimos to central African rain-forest pygmies and Manhattan city dwellers—are much more similar genetically than had ever been thought or would have been expected on the basis of external appearances and cultural comparisons alone. These lines of human DNA study, along with the growing support of the fossil record, are providing a solid scientific underpinning to the contention that we are all made "in the image of God" as "brothers and sisters under the skin"!

Brains, Language, and DNA

While differences in the basic biology and genetic make-up of diverse groups of our human species may not be as great as had once been thought, the same is not true of the third and final feature that sets our human selves apart from all other living creatures, namely, the development of a complex spoken language. Interestingly, connections between the Broca region of the brain and the frontal regions of the brain, where abstract thoughts are processed, are responsible for both language and manual skills. The early embryonic development of these brain regions, which show disproportionate development in those primate lines that lead to man, are under the control of a particular family of genes. Current research is investigating the possibility that an alteration in the genetic code pre-adapted an ancestral *Homo habilis* or *Homo erectus* to acquire both unique anatomical structures (for example, an agile, opposable thumb) and associated neural circuits. These circuits permitted the development of complex and hierarchical skills in both spoken language and tool-making and use.[18]

Studies of the fossil record suggest that the vocal apparatus of archaic humans of the Neanderthal type was incapable of making the complex series of sounds required to string words together into intelligible speech. That skill seems to have been acquired only as a result of the unique placement of the larynx and epiglottis characteristic of the modern-type humans that were emerging from the Africa of our mitochondrial Eve, 100,000 to 200,000 years ago.

Indeed, it has been conjectured that such superior language skills were a telling factor both in allowing modern-type humans to outcompete and eventually replace their Neanderthal-type contemporaries, and in reducing the likelihood of interbreeding between them.[19] Even today, language differences often represent the major barrier to gene flow between human groups. In contrast, geographic barriers, such as mountain ranges or bodies of water, more commonly act to restrict gene flow between potentially interbreeding groups of other species of animals.

Initial language barriers to gene flow between human groups would have tended to reinforce themselves, since the sharing of a common linguistic and cultural heritage is an extremely important factor in mate choice within our species. As linguistically defined and genetically isolated units migrated into regions occupied by other groups, these barriers would have worked against interbreeding, further establishing and increasing the genetic diversity of our species as a whole.[20]

We have thus now come full circle: the DNA genetic code is involved in the establishment and development of the ability to use a complex spoken language, and linguistic ability has in turn increased the fragmentation and diversification of ethnic groups, and therefore of the genetic code of our species.

Preserving Human Genomes

The importance of genetic variability as a factor promoting long-term population viability and well-being has been well-established.[21] Captive breeding programs designed to help save endangered species are carefully designed to ensure that as little genetic variability as possible is lost from one generation to the next.[22]

In the case of human populations, however, there has been less of a case for identifying and preserving genetic variability. While genetic variability allows a population to adapt to environmental change, in modern civilizations, the direct impact of most environmental changes (for example, climate alteration) is ameliorated through short-term technological "fixes" (such as insulated housing, modern heating systems, and air-conditioning). Even in the area of health and susceptibility to disease, advantageous genetic mutations that confer resistance to various parasites and pathogens now fail to confer significant advantages. In most technologically advanced human societies, access to antibiotics and other benefits of modern medicine obviates the need for specific disease-resistant genetic variants to enhance the likelihood of survival and production of offspring.

In less technologically-advanced human societies, such genetic variants have often been beneficial, but sometimes with a cost that only later became apparent. The variant gene causing the sickle-cell trait in African Americans, for example, also conferred resistance to malaria and was thus favored in ancestral tropical populations. In temperate North America, however, this gene no longer conferred a selective advantage to its bearers. Rather, they began to be subject to the counterbalancing negative effects of sickle-cell anemia.[23]

Thus, as Africans came to reside in malaria-free areas, the previous advantage conferred by this genetic trait was transformed into a heritable biochemical liability. Similarly, the gene causing Tay-Sachs disease, which occurs with higher frequency among American Jews of European descent, is thought to have conferred a degree of resistance to the epidemics of tuberculosis that once swept through European ghettos.[24]

As these two examples suggest, whether a particular genetic variant will be an asset or a liability depends on the particular environmental conditions and even more importantly on the way these conditions change over time. If we are to understand how this process of genetic adaptation to environmental change will affect us in the future, we must understand better how it worked as modern *Homo sapiens* emerged from Africa, diversified, and became ethnically and culturally adapted to the broad spectrum of climates and living conditions found on earth today.

This process has obviously served our species well, as we see by *Homo sapiens'* notable success in populating (and, unfortunately, often overpopulating) the far reaches of this planet. An important step in gaining a better understanding of this process would be to survey and document—in as precise a molecular genetic language as possible—the entire spectrum of human genetic variability as it presently exists.

Such work has a certain urgency, since a number of factors now threaten the ethnic and cultural diversity of our species. As the influence of the superpower nations spreads across the globe, loss of human genetic diversity seems inevitable. Cross-cultural and trans-regional marriages increase, and pockets of uniquely isolated primitive peoples (and their attendant unique languages and cultures) either die out or are assimilated into larger invading ethnic groups.

The overall impact of this process of cultural and genetic assimilation depends on the scale of invasion and genetic contact between groups. Limited genetic exchanges between otherwise isolated population subgroups can actually enhance overall population genetic variability.[25] When large-scale genetic swamping occurs, however, unique genetic combinations found in smaller subgroups are lost, thus resulting in a loss of overall population genome diversity.

We have no other source of information than these diverse human genomes to show us how human genes interact with, and may be changed by, diverse environments. Accordingly, a number of anthropologists and human geneticists have now called for establishing and preserving a DNA-based record of our species' total genetic diversity for future scientific study and interpretation: a Human **Genomes** Project (as opposed to the Human Genome Project).[26]

Also known as the Human Genome Diversity Project, the Human Genomes Project involves collecting blood samples and, through molecular genetic technology, establishing and preserving "genomic libraries." The genomic libraries would collect the unique DNA genetic profiles of the world's diverse ethnic groups, particularly those that have been reduced in number and/or threatened with imminent extinction or cultural assimilation. Cell lines containing the DNA of at least twenty-five individuals from each sampled population would be established from blood samples drawn in the field and cultured in the laboratory to produce sufficient DNA for future research needs.[27]

The better-known Human Genome Project is now commanding a significant proportion of our society's scientific personnel and resources. It is providing, however, only a single consensus "snapshot" of the human genetic code, and no information on the variability that has developed within that code over the millions of years of our evolution and adaptation to our earth's changing environments.

The complementary process of finding and preserving samples of our species' far-flung genetic diversity represents our only hope of saving the entire panorama of genetic codes. A complete record of the genetic "literature" might help us define what it really means to be human, and to be made "in the image of God." These libraries of stored genetic codes will almost certainly help us define a more enlightened course for our future development.[28]

NOTES

1. Robert Pollack, *Signs of Life: The Language and Meanings of DNA* (New York: Houghton Mifflin, 1994), 33.

2. John Tierney, Lynda Wright, and Karen Springen, "The Search for Adam and Eve," *Newsweek* 111 (January 11, 1988): 46–52.

3. Elwyn L. Simons, "Human Origins," *Science* 245 (1989): 1343–1349.

4. Bernd Herrmann and Susanne Hummel, eds., *Ancient DNA: Recovery and Analysis of Genetic Material from Paleontological, Archaeological, Museum, Medical, and Forensic Specimens* (New York: Springer-Verlag, 1994).

5. Pollack, 160.

6. Geoffrey Cowley, "The Roots of Good and Evil—What Can Chimps Tell Us About Our Moral Nature?" *Newsweek* 127 (February 26, 1996): 52–54.

7. Jeffrey Moussaieff Masson and Susan McCarthy, *When Elephants Weep* (New York: Dell, 1995), 96–97. Additional striking visual documentation

is provided in the video production, "Reflections on Elephants," (Washington, D.C.: National Geographic Television, 1994).

8. Ralph S. Solecki, "Shanidar IV, a Neanderthal Flower Burial in Northern Iraq," *Science* 190 (1975): 880-881.

9. Pollack, 162–165.

10. Roy Larick and Russell L. Ciochon, "The African Emergence and Early Asian Dispersals of the Genus *Homo,*" *American Scientist* 84 (1996): 538–551.

11. Pollack, 160–162.

12. Wilma Mankiller (Cherokee Scholar and Principal Chief of the Cherokee Nation), in "The Native Americans: Tribes of the Southeast— Persistent Cultures of Resilient People," Video Production (Atlanta: Turner Broadcasting Systems Productions, 1994).

13. Gina Bari Kolata, "The Demise of the Neandertals: Was Language a Factor?" *Science* 186 (1974): 618–619; and Ann Gibbons, "Paleoanthropology: Did Neandertals Lose an Evolutionary 'Arms' Race?" *Science* 272 (1996): 1586–1587.

14. Roger Lewin, "Modern Human Origins under Close Scrutiny," *Science* 239 (1988): 1240–1241.

15. Francisco J. Ayala, "The Myth of Eve: Molecular Biology and Human Origins," *Science* 270 (1995): 1930–1936; Ann Gibbons, "Looking for the Father of Us All," *Science* 251 (1991): 378–380; and Joshua Fischman, "Molecular Evolution: Evidence Mounts for Our African Origins— and Alternatives," *Science* 271 (1996): 1364.

16. Tierney, Wright, and Springen, 46–52.

17. Ayala, 1933–1934.

18. Pollack, 162–165.

19. Kolata, 618–619.

20. Pollack, 165–170.

21. John C. Avise and James L. Hamrick, eds., *Conservation Genetics: Case Histories from Nature* (New York: Chapman & Hall, 1996).

22. Ronald K. Chesser, Michael H. Smith, and I. Lehr Brisbin, Jr., "Management and Maintenance of Genetic Variability in Endangered Species," *International Zoo Yearbook* 20 (1980): 146–154.

23. Pollack, 39–40, 48, 50, 51n.

24. Pollack, 51n.

25. Chesser, Smith, and Brisbin, 146–154.

26. Pollack, 172–173.

27. Anna Maria Gillis, "Getting a Picture of Human Diversity," *BioScience* 44 (1994): 8–11; Leslie Roberts, "Molecular Anthropology: How to

Sample the World's Genetic Diversity," *Science* 257 (1992): 1204–1205; and Leslie Roberts, "Genome Diversity Project: Anthropologists Climb (Gingerly) on Board," *Science* 258 (1992): 1300–1301.

28. I am grateful to Cham Dallas, Bob Wentworth, Jeri Perkins, and Bill Johnston for encouraging my thinking about these issues. Fatimah Jackson, Bruce Eberhardt, and Henry Gurr provided critical readings of the manuscript. Support associated with manuscript preparation was provided by Financial Assistance Award No. DE-FC09-96SR18546 from the U.S. Department of Energy to the University of Georgia Research Foundation.

Summary

Combined with advances in archaeology and in our understanding of animal behavior, molecular genetics is helping to give us a fuller picture of human evolutionary history. We are increasingly aware of our similarity to many animals, especially the great apes, even in questions of consciousness. Analysis of DNA from fossils that are thousands of years old has also helped us better to understand the emergence of humans from, and along with, other human-like species.

Furthermore, DNA research has established that humans are much more similar to each other genetically than differences of appearance and culture might suggest. Yet the capacity for language, which is based to a great extent in our genetic code, has simultaneously resulted in greater diversification of the gene pool than would have occurred otherwise. Differences in language have separated different ethnic groups from each other; in some cases, these groups also have distinctive genetic characteristics reflecting their adaptation to particular environments.

If we are to appreciate what it means to be created in the image of God, we must better understand this genetic diversity. Some scientists are now calling for an effort to record our species' total genetic library, with particular attention to ethnic groups that are threatened with extinction or cultural assimilation.

Study Questions

1. What signs of a "spiritual life" do we find in some of the great apes? How do you feel about claims that they may have a soul?
2. It is possible that scientists could someday produce a living hybrid of a human and a higher primate. Would such a creature have a soul? Would such a creature be eligible to receive God's gift of salvation?
3. The history of life on earth and the history of our own species' evolution suggest that humans continue to evolve. What are the implications for our theology if we have reason to think that humankind as we know it will someday pass away or be replaced as the most advanced form of life?

4. How do you react to the notion that humans and animals are closely related genetically? Does this correspondence support the concerns of the animal rights movement?

5. How do the results of DNA research confirm or challenge the church's understanding that we are all "children of God"?

PART III

WHAT GOD CREATED US TO BE

Chapter 6

Biblical and Theological Perspectives on the Human Condition

Susan L. Nelson

The Dilemma of Human Self-Understanding

Riding the metro in Washington, D.C., a few days after Christmas, I was struck by a billboard that greeted riders at every station: "We never forget there's a human in each human body. Georgetown University Medical Center." The billboard seemed to promise readers that the advertiser's medical system would treat each client as more than a body. It seemed to suggest that something called "a human" is "in" each human body.

These words captured my attention because it was Christmastide, when Christians celebrate the incarnation and announce to the world that God's Word dared to become flesh, a human person. I wondered about the notion that humans are "in" their bodies, almost as if whatever characterizes our humanity is something different from our bodies. What *does* it mean to be *human*? What does the Bible tell us about that "something" that characterizes our humanity? Would a biblical view say that humans are *in* their bodies?

The difficulty in looking to the Bible for an answer to the age-old dilemma of human self-understanding is that the Bible is not a textbook. It is rather a library of diverse materials that tell about a select grouping of people and their relationships with their God. Scripture gives us a picture, but not a systematic presentation, of the human condition.

Moreover, scripture offers not just one story of the human predicament. Scripture weaves together many strands of tradition, some of which stand in tension. The picture of the human condition that emerges is complex and ambiguous. It is drawn from the lives of specific people in specific historical and social circumstances.

Nonetheless, scripture is the church's book, a source of memory and promise by which the church lives. Within scripture's diversity, we find prominent themes that help us to make sense of our humanity.

Meaning Makers, and Yet . . .

O LORD . . . what are human beings that you are mindful of them, mortals that you care for them? (Psalm 8:4)

To be human is to wonder, to ask questions, to want to know why things are and who we are in the midst of all that is. Emerging from a concentration camp as a survivor of Nazi brutality, holocaust survivor Viktor Frankl wrote *Man's Search for Meaning*.[1] In seeking to make sense of the human condition in the context of such horror, Frankl put himself in a long line of human beings who have demanded to know who we are and how God's purpose is reflected in the reality of our existence.

The Bible pictures human beings searching for knowledge; trying to make sense of life and death; asking how periods of captivity or wandering factor into the meaning of history and life; calling God to account when evil threatens their understanding of reality; holding to a covenant from God as the foundation stone for their self-understanding, and as a guide for their life together; and encoding strands of their wisdom traditions into their holy remembrance. To be human is to search for meaning and to seek to construct our lives in meaningful ways.

Yet the human beings of whom we read in the Bible also face limits to their wisdom. The story of the Garden in Genesis 3 raises questions about the human quest for knowledge: of power (Who controls the knowledge? Who makes the meaning?); of right relationship to the source of all meaning (Do human meanings accept or reject

God's structure of meaning?); and of right relationship with oneself, others, and the world (Do humans turn their knowledge against one another? Do they use it rightly to know themselves? Does the knowledge that they use for their own purposes risk the well-being of all creation?).

God challenges human wisdom, for instance, when God addresses Job out of the whirlwind, "Who is this that darkens counsel by words without knowledge?" (Job 38:2). And Jesus in his parables constantly upsets the human understandings of his followers. (The prodigal is, after all, welcomed home [Luke 15:11–32], and all the laborers in the vineyard are paid the same wage [Matthew 20:1–16].)

Moreover, the meaning that some biblical characters finally gain and accept for their lives transcends human understanding. In the midst of travail that makes no sense to him, Habakkuk proclaims, "Though the fig tree does not blossom, and no fruit is on the vines . . . yet I will rejoice in the Lord" (Habakkuk 3:17–18). Habakkuk (like Job) discovers and accepts a new logic that reaches beyond his understanding.

Creatures in a Creation

According to the poet William Wordsworth, human beings are born "trailing clouds of glory."[2] This image suggests that our bodies have captured a bit of divinity. The biblical vision of humanity is more "down to earth." The first human creature in the Bible is "adam" (of the earth), created from the dust of the earth. Although those first creatures were animated by the breath of God (suggesting that they are not just dust, but enlivened dust, with vitality and freedom and spirit), they were clearly not God. To be human is to be created, of finite "stuff" (and thereby subject to suffering, disease, hunger, and death, and dependent upon a Creator).

But the term "creation" is theologically loaded. It refers not only to the existence of earth and nature but also to the value, order, and meaning of all that is created. To say that there is a creation is to say that there is a Creator upon whom the creation is dependent and from whom it garners meaning. To speak of creation is to say that our life and the order of nature of which we are a part are purposeful, valued, and good.

If humans are created, their lives are characterized not only by contingency and vulnerability, but also by blessing. Whereas some philosophical movements have suggested that the earth, nature, and human bodiliness are a curse, a form of bondage for an immortal soul, a biblical view of humanity counters that the world is God's creation; even in its limitations, its struggles, and its sufferings, it is good.

The term "creation" also suggests that human beings are not something different from "nature" (in contrast to what our opening quotation seems to suggest) but *are* nature. Even if human beings have consciousness and a sense of themselves as not only nature but also something more, they do not stand outside nature. Rather, as John F. Haught has suggested, human beings are nature coming to consciousness.[3]

The term "creation" also suggests that human existence has a relational character. Life is a web of inter-connectivity where the ill- or well-being of one part affects the totality. Scripture affirms that we are individuals. We are not identical to our community. Yet our individuality includes the desire and ability to be in relationship with one another. In Genesis 2, the only thing that was not good in all of creation was aloneness. (We read: "And then the LORD God said, 'It is not good that the man should be alone'" [Genesis 2:18a].)

In scripture, relations precede individuals. The covenant with a people names and shapes the individuals who belong to that people. Human beings are born as part of a community, formed and known through their communities, and named in the context of their families and their histories (thus the endless genealogies and the retelling of ancient stories as a ground of meaning and hope). Human beings yearn for face-to-face relations (Ruth accompanies Naomi; Jonathan longs for David) and are miserable when cut off from one another (Cain wanders alone in the wilderness; the sick and the sinners need healing that will restore them to community; those who are barren and thus without hope for giving life to a new generation call themselves forgotten.)

Far from the individualistic mentality of the Western worldview, scripture offers a vision of a creation whose parts are intertwined (so that all creation suffers with the sins of humanity, and all creation groans for redemption [Romans 8:19–23]). The comings and goings of individuals are not unrelated; rather, one's sufferings can be understood as representing the community's (see Isaiah 52 and 53 where the prophet acknowledges that the servant suffers for the community's sins, not simply for his own). The community is the locus of redemption (and so God redeems a remnant of the people of Israel, not just particular individuals). The body of Christ is the *koinonia* (community, communion) of believers.[4] Ultimately, we are in community with a Creator. To be cut off from that Creator is to feel as if life and breath are threatened (Psalm 104:27–30).

At times, scripture assumes a hierarchical ordering of relationships. The nonhuman part of creation serves human needs. Among humans, men are the principal carriers of value (created, perhaps, more in the image of God than are women). But scripture also has a vision of relationality that undermines hierarchy. Nature is not simply a tool for human use; it reflects the glory of God and is in need of human stewardship. Whereas much of the Christian tradition remembered Eve as created second and subordinate to Adam, Genesis 2 itself suggests that God created them to live in mutuality and complementarity.[5] And scripture testifies to Jesus as one who upset traditional hierarchies. He announced that the last should be first, and that the greatest should serve the least. He welcomed women and other outsiders into his circle of fellowship.

In "the Image," but Not As Central As We Would Like

Genesis 1:27 tells us that humans were created in the image of God; Genesis 2 pictures humanity as the center of creation around whom and for whom the rest of creation exists. The Christian doctrine of salvation, the proclamation that Jesus came to save all humanity, pictures human creatures and human salvation as the central concern of God (despite the view of Romans 8 that God intends the redemption of *all* creation).

What does it mean to be created in God's image? Christian tradition has been divided in its answer. For some, "image" refers to human rationality as somehow mirroring the order and reason of God that we see in the order of creation. For others, "image" refers to human sovereignty and responsibility, that is, the power of humans to name the rest of creation and to stand as God's representatives in the ongoing stewardship of creation.

Others believe that "image" points to human self-transcendence and the human ability to imagine and thus draw close to God, while others assert that "image" is not something innate in the isolated individual, but refers to the relationality (the for- and with-the-otherness) that is the fullest expression of a human being.

These understandings of the image of God probably reflect personal values as well as the social constructions of different times. Yet this biblical imagery seems to be consistent in suggesting some kind of correspondence between the human and the divine, some kind of relationality to the divine that is central to the human, and a sense that humanity and human well-being are central to the process of creation.

While scripture affirms the value and centrality of humanity in the story of creation, it also pictures human beings as more limited and less significant than they might sometimes wish. The people of Israel understood themselves to be God's elect. They understood their story of exile and return to be central to God's plans for the world. Yet God had elected them not solely for their own sake, but also to bear responsibility for the salvation of the world. ("I will give you as a light to the nations" [Isaiah 49:6].)

At times, God is pictured as concerned for the people of other lands (such as Nineveh, in the story of Jonah), even though the people of Israel thought that they were the center of the world. Jesus repeatedly seeks fellowship with those traditionally excluded from the circle of the righteous (see, for example, Luke 5:29–32), and he reminds the people of a God who cares even for the sparrows and the lilies (Matthew 6:26, 28). Peter is led through a dream to embrace the gentile Cornelius as part of the family of God (Acts 9—10).

Moreover, the Bible reflects an awareness from time to time that God delights not only in humans, but in the whole of creation. This perspective on the world and its value is more theocentric (God-centered) than anthropocentric (human-centered).

A human-centered valuing of creation would likely focus on the fact that Leviathan, the sea monster, was terrifying to human beings. But Psalm 104 pictures Leviathan as "sporting" in the sea and enjoying itself, as though simply to the glory of God. And, in the book of

Job, God answers Job's accusations with a series of questions. God amazes Job not only with God's power and knowledge of every part of creation, but also with God's concern to value it apart from any value that humans might assign it. ("Is it by your wisdom that the hawk soars? . . . Is it at your command that the eagle mounts up?" [Job 39:26–27].)

In sum, scripture knows humans to be made in God's image and to hold a central place in the story of creation. But it also challenges human beings to reconsider their sense of self-importance.

Humans as Embodied

We have already spoken about human beings as created and in creation. Yet the Christian tradition has sometimes held ambivalent attitudes toward the human body. We must therefore emphasize again that human beings, as understood in the Bible, are not "in" bodies, but in fact "are" bodies.[6] To be human is to have hungers and desires, to have passions, to long for sexual expression, to need touch (and to glory in it when it is given), and to know oneself as gendered—male or female.

This intuition that human beings are bodies is clearly expressed in Genesis 2, where the first creatures are ecstatic with one another, are pictured in a garden that delights their senses, and are told that they might enjoy that garden (within certain limits) and each other. The fact that humans are embodied creatures is also apparent as Jesus receives the tears of a woman who washes his feet. It is whispered in the Song of Songs, where lovers take delight in one another, and in the thanksgiving of the community for times of harvest and well-being, which provide for their physical needs. It echoes in the affirmation of the resurrection of the *body* (and not some disembodied soul) and in the proclamation of the Word made flesh.

The fact that humans are embodied also means that humans are self-interested, vulnerable to hurt, and capable of hurting others. Humans can lose control of their passions (witness Cain and Abel, or David and Bathsheba). Humans can be so concerned for feeding their own bodies that they forget about the needs of others (as the stories of Lazarus [Luke 16:19–31] and the rich fool who fruitlessly builds storage bins to secure his existence [Luke 12:16–21] demonstrate). They can become so consumed with worry or anguish that even the beauteous creation becomes flat and meaningless to them, and their lives intolerable (Job 10:1).

Humans love and know the glory of that love, and they suffer the pain of loss. (Think of the many parents in the Bible who plead for the healing of their sick or dead children. Witness the tears of Jesus and Mary and Martha at the death of his friend and their brother Lazarus [John 11:35].) To be human is to be embodied, to know the delights of the body, and to be vulnerable to the suffering that bodies in their dependency and finitude give and receive.

To Long for Something More: Spirit, Sin, and the Reign of God

Traditionally, scholars have spoken of a tripartite biblical anthropology, which is a fancy way of saying that humans have body, soul, and spirit. Whereas body (the fact that we are embodied creatures) is fairly apparent to us, soul and spirit are not. Scripture understands soul to refer to the enlivening aspect of human embodiment (the breath of life), and spirit to the experience of self-transcendence (the awareness of self and of "something more" to life). All three are understood to be inseparable from one another. Their bonds are not dissolved until death—and even then traditional Christian teaching about the resurrection foresaw their reunification (thus, the resurrection of the *body*).

While specific communities, bodies, historical contexts, and places help to define humans, humans are not just subject to biological/historical destiny. Scripture also sees humans as *free*. The first creature names the other animals, thereby suggesting the human ability to create and have power over parts of creation. Humans can free themselves from the constraints of historical and familial obligations. Abram leaves the land of his father and mother, and follows a call to found a new nation (Genesis 12:1–5). Jesus' followers were to leave the dead to bury the dead (Matthew 8:21–22), and James and John were to leave their boat and father (Matthew 4:21–22).

Scripture also testifies to those who from time to time experience themselves as being "something more" or belonging to "something more." Biblical figures are often aware of the vulnerability of their existence, as when the psalmists and Job question God out of the midst of their pain. Scripture affirms that humans have a conscience and the possibility for moral existence, as when God gives the people of Israel the Ten Commandments (Exodus 20). Scripture knows that humans judge themselves and one another (Romans 7:15). They long not just to know, but to love and to be loved. They search for, hear, and follow a God whom they understand as holy and distinct from themselves—a God who knows them, and who calls them into new ways of living and loving and knowing.

Scripture tells of those who cry out for deliverance from times of trial, reveals their ability to envision a new heaven and earth and a realm of justice, and describes their quest for meaning. Humans search for (and are confronted by) the ground of their meaning (to borrow from and expand upon one of Paul Tillich's symbols for God).[7] They have freedom (within the constraints of creation and history) to determine who they are, whom they will worship, and whether they will dare to believe that they might be friends of God.

Thus, scripture sees human beings as persons of spirit who have the possibility to choose God. To be human is to have the freedom to affect others and the responsibility to do so carefully. To be human is to have the possibility of loving someone other than oneself, to be loyal, and to cling to meanings for which rational explanation is elusive. But to be human is also to be capable of great abuses of freedom. To be human, says the Bible, is to sin.

The Bible sometimes understands sin as *acts* of violating the good. Humans miss the mark. They adopt postures of defiance and despair, disobey God's intentions ("law"), and practice deceit, hardness of heart, and idolatry.

But the Bible also understands sin as a *condition*. It is a *consciousness* that one has missed the mark. One experiences a "dividedness," where one knows the good but anguishes over not doing it. One is aware of one's impotence to change oneself and choose what is best. One realizes one's complicity in the sufferings of others.

While the Bible offers no systematically developed doctrine of original sin, it does suggest that this distortion of the human condition is paralyzing, is passed on through the generations as children learn their parents' sinful ways, and is universal (even if creation itself is good). To be sure, scripture pictures many acts of human love, loyalty, courage, faithfulness, and compassion. The good Samaritan behaves in an ethical and compassionate way, even if the others do not (Luke 10:29–37). The mother in Solomon's court who relinquishes her child, rather than allow it to be cut in two, reflects a choice to love and keep trust when the world offers horrible choices (1 Kings 3:16–28).

But scripture also attests to the human ability to deny obligations, to violate the humanity of others, and to commit gross acts of betrayal. (While Judas is the classic example, scripture is littered with stories of betrayal. The killing of Jephthah's daughter is one such "text of terror" [Judges 11:29–40].)[8] In a desperate effort to secure themselves, people are capable of great treachery (thus Jephthah's oath to Yahweh [Judges 11:30–31], Cain's response to Abel [Genesis 4:8–9], and Herod's killing of the newborn males [Matthew 2:16]).

As the prophets continually remind us, human beings, individually and communally, do miss the mark. They often numb themselves to others' miseries or blame the victim, rather than seeing and resisting injustice. Isaiah tells Israel that it is for the sins of the community that the suffering servant dies, not for anything that he has done to deserve such treatment (Isaiah 53:7–9).

And humans often choose safe old ways over new uncertain ones that God offers them. The children of Israel, we remember, longed to return to the slavery of Egypt rather than wander in the wilderness.

Imperiled, Yet Blessed: Yearning for God

Thus, the Bible pictures human beings as living a life that is both blessed (there is the beauty of the earth, the delight of love, the fruitfulness of families, the hope of the generations, the experience of healing and of restoration to community) and imperiled. Created for a garden, human beings find themselves in a wilderness, where life knows toil and pain. While scripture does not use wilderness as a totally negative metaphor, the term does capture the sense that life is not always easy, and that human beings are often at enmity with others, themselves, and the very land on which they live.[9]

Yet scripture understands human beings also as a people of hope. They not only work to feed themselves (and suffer in times of famine and drought), but are given manna, bread for the journey

(Exodus 16). They may treat each other wretchedly, but they also know to welcome the stranger and care for the widow and orphan. They see that grass withers and flowers fade (fragility, after all, is part of what makes beauty so excruciatingly lovely), and yet they continue to marvel at creation while believing that there is something—the Word of God—that endures forever (Isaiah 40:6–8).

Scripture teaches us to recognize, and to make sense of, the vicissitudes of life. Humans know slavery, exile, destruction, and murder, and yet they can tell their story as salvation history—as the story of God's covenant with and care for a people. They know that life is fleeting and yearn to make their life more secure, and yet they can treasure moments of blessing, as did Mary, the mother of Jesus (Luke 2:51b). Scripture offers us the promise that we can greet life with open arms, trusting that there is a God whose face shines upon us and whose love will not let us go.

And So?

This biblical view of humanity can inform our dialogue with the sciences. The sciences can remind us that we are a marvelous conjoining of body and soul. We are embodied, relational, and interdependent. We are shaped by genetic codes, family histories, and inherited knowledge. Our community and our historical context help to define us.

But human beings are not just subject to destiny. We are also blessed with spirit, that is, with conscience and the possibility to lead a moral life; with compassion and the possibility to create caring and healing communities; with intelligence and the power to name and create the world in new ways (for example, through the disciplines of science); with visions of justice and life for a better world than the one we know; and with some capability to reflect on the meaning of life.

Yet our possibilities and freedom are always hedged in. Our finitude, our limited ability to know, our dependence upon forces beyond our control, our tendency to use our knowledge in ways that are more self-serving than we might admit, and our capacity for treachery, learned ignorance, and rationalization—each of these factors reminds us to exercise care as we develop new technologies (which is a gift of our creativity), and as we long for a better world and seek to understand the intricacies of the many forces that shape this world.

We need to develop the discipline of hearing the concerns of all people (especially those upon whom our new technologies may trample). We need to acknowledge our creatureliness and our dependence on the One who is our source and our destiny (our Alpha and Omega, as scripture tells us). We need to remember that we are bodies and not just mind or spirit. And we need to watch for, and repent of, all the ways in which we (as members of an intricately interconnected creation) will inevitably be complicit in the suffering and misery of others, despite our best intentions.

NOTES

1. Viktor E. Frankl, *Man's Search for Meaning* (New York: Washington Square, 1963).

2. William Wordsworth, "Intimations of Immortality," *Complete Poetical Works of William Wordsworth,* ed. Henry Reed (Philadelphia: Hayes and Zell, 1854), 470–71.

3. John F. Haught, "Religious and Cosmic Homelessness: Some Environmental Implications," *Liberating Life: Contemporary Approaches to Ecological Theology,* ed. Charles Birch, William Eakin, Jay B. McDaniel (Maryknoll, N.Y.: Orbis, 1990), 159–181.

4. The use of body imagery for the community of believers (for example, 1 Corinthians 12:12–27) also suggests the interdependence of this community.

5. Phyllis Trible, "A Love Story Gone Awry," *God and the Rhetoric of Sexuality* (Philadelphia: Fortress, 1978), 72–143.

6. While the unity of body and soul are fundamental to the Old Testament understanding of the human being, New Testament authors—probably reflecting Hellenistic influence—understood the soul as "opposed to body and considered immortal." See W. E. Lynch, "Soul (in the Bible)," *New Catholic Encyclopedia,* vol. XIII (New York: McGraw Hill, 1967), 449–450.

7. Paul Tillich, *The Courage To Be* (New Haven, Conn.: Yale University Press, 1952).

8. Phyllis Trible, *Texts of Terror* (Philadelphia: Fortress, 1984), 93–116.

9. For wilderness as a positive metaphor, see Delores S. Williams, *Sisters in the Wilderness* (Maryknoll, N.Y.: Orbis, 1993).

Summary

Scripture identifies several key tensions that characterize the human condition. First, humans seek meaning for their lives, yet human wisdom is always limited and incomplete. God may even call us to a way of life that goes beyond our understanding. Second, as created in the image of God, humans are uniquely related to God, yet we are also limited, vulnerable, and dependent, situated both in nature and in communities that shape us. We are central to creation, yet not always as important as we would like to believe. Third, humans are bodies (not just "in" bodies), yet we also have spirit. We are aware of, and long for, "something more" to life. Fourth, humans are free, yet we inevitably violate the good, betray each other, and fail to love and keep trust.

These tensions help to inform our dialogue with the sciences. We are subject to the forces of nature and history that the sciences help to describe, but we are also creatures that depend ultimately on God. We can misuse the knowledge and power that the sciences provide, but we can also use them to understand the forces that shape our world, so that we might seek a better world.

Study Questions

1. How much knowledge is a good thing? Are there some things that we should not try to know?
2. What does it mean to be "created"? How are humans different from, and similar to, other "creatures"?
3. The capacity for, and longing for, relationship is central to human life. What kinds of relationships sustain us? What can we learn from Jesus about the kinds of relationships to which God calls us?
4. How should we treat our bodies? To what degree do they define us? To what degree are we something more than our bodies?
5. We often find it difficult to live in the tensions that characterize the human condition. We are tempted to think too much of ourselves, or too little; to deny our bodies, or to deny our spirits; to be too independent, or too dependent. How do you see yourself struggling with these tensions? How does our society acknowledge or deny these tensions?

6. What can the sciences teach us about the human condition? What can we as Christians teach society about the sciences and both their possibilities and limitations?

7. How does the Bible speak to the human condition? Why is it more like a collection of stories than a textbook? How do we deal with the tensions in scripture?

Chapter 7

Human Nature, the Soul, and Sin: A Look at Reformed Confessions

James C. Goodloe IV

The Church's Confessions

A brief historical summary of the Reformed and Presbyterian doctrines of humanity, the soul, and sin may help us to reflect more thoughtfully on questions of faith and science, including current discussions of evolution, a historical understanding of the world and life, and genetic engineering and human nature.[1] Because the church's understanding and articulation of its faith and doctrine have changed and developed, especially in response to particular historical challenges, no single statement, nor the sum of them, is either a complete or final statement of the Christian faith. Nonetheless, these creeds, confessions, catechisms, declarations, and statements "guide the church in its study and interpretation of the scriptures; they summarize the essence of Christian tradition; they direct the church in maintaining sound doctrine; they equip the church for its work of proclamation."[2]

The Doctrine of Humanity

It is striking and significant that the church's confessions have a good deal more to say about God than about humanity. From the Reformed perspective, this emphasis is appropriate. The church and its confessions are more concerned to praise God than to explicate the human condition. The Westminster Shorter Catechism begins with the famous question and answer, "What is the chief end of man? Man's chief end is to glorify God, and to enjoy him forever."[3] Humanity's ultimate purpose is to worship and to delight in God.

The fundamental distinction here is between God the Creator and God's creatures. Hence the opening words of the Nicene Creed: "We believe in one God the Father Almighty, Maker of heaven and earth, and of all things visible and invisible."[4] This emphasis runs throughout the confessions.[5] God is God, and we are not.

At the same time, humans cannot be fully understood apart from God. If God is Creator, human life did not emerge by chance or accident but by the will and purpose of God.[6] Humans are not alone. The Heidelberg Catechism states this understanding of humanity with particular warmth:

> **Q. 1.** What is your only comfort, in life and in death?
> **A.** That I belong—body and soul, in life and in death—not to myself but to my faithful Savior, Jesus Christ, who at the cost of his own blood has fully paid for all my sins and has completely freed me from the dominion of the devil; that he protects me so well that without the will of my Father in heaven not a hair can fall from my head; indeed, that everything must fit his purpose for my salvation. Therefore, by his Holy Spirit, he also assures me of eternal life, and makes me wholeheartedly willing and ready from now on to live for him.
>
> **Q. 26.** What do you believe when you say, "I believe in God the Father Almighty, Maker of heaven and earth"?
> **A.** That the eternal Father of our Lord Jesus Christ, who out of nothing created heaven and earth with all that is in them, who also upholds and governs them by his eternal counsel and providence, is for the sake of Christ his Son my God and my Father. I trust in him so completely that I have no doubt that he will provide me with all things necessary for body and soul. Moreover, whatever evil he sends upon me in this troubled life he will turn to my good, for he is able to do it,

being almighty God, and is determined to do it, being a faithful Father.

Q. 27. What do you understand by the providence of God?
A. The almighty and ever-present power of God whereby he still upholds, as it were by his own hand, heaven and earth together with all creatures, and rules in such a way that leaves and grass, rain and drought, fruitful and unfruitful years, food and drink, health and sickness, riches and poverty, and everything else, come to us not by chance but by his fatherly hand.

Q. 28. What advantage comes from acknowledging God's creation and providence?
A. We learn that we are to be patient in adversity, grateful in the midst of blessing, and to trust our faithful God and Father for the future, assured that no creature shall separate us from his love, since all creatures are so completely in his hand that without his will they cannot even move.[7]

As a consequence of this distinction between the Creator and the creatures, we can learn a great deal about the nature of humanity by contrasting it with the nature of God. To turn to the Shorter Catechism again, "What is God? God is a Spirit, infinite, eternal, and unchangeable, in his being, wisdom, power, holiness, justice, goodness, and truth."[8] This statement implies that humans are bodily, finite, temporal, and changeable, hence limited in being, wisdom, power, holiness, justice, goodness, and truth. These limits are profound givens of the human situation, realities that will never be overcome. We have only so much strength, breath, time, life, intelligence, goodness, and resources.

But classic Christian doctrine not only distinguishes us from God, it also relates us to God. Even though we are limited in time, space, and resources, we can to some extent transcend our finitude. We can imagine that we are in another time and place, or that we possess other resources.

Moreover, we are not only conscious, but self-conscious. This self-consciousness is part (though only part) of what it means to say that we are created in the image of God (see Genesis 1:28). The Scots Confession lists a variety of attributes and characteristics:

> We confess and acknowledge that our God has created man, i.e., our first father, Adam, after his own image and likeness, to whom he gave wisdom, lordship, justice, free will, and self-consciousness, so that in the whole nature of man no imperfection could be found.[9]

Thus, we are created in the image of God, so that we may be in a special relationship with God. As the Heidelberg Catechism says: "God created man good and in his image, that is, in true righteousness and holiness, so that he might rightly know God his Creator, love him with his whole heart, and live with him in eternal blessedness, praising and glorifying him."[10]

In sum, a human being is a *created* being, hence finite. But it is also created in the *image of God.* It has the transcendent capacity and express purpose of being in relationship with God.

The Doctrine of the Soul

The confessions discuss the human soul within the context of the creation of human beings in the image of God. We need here to make a careful distinction. While creation in the image of God is best understood as a person's *capacity* for being in a special relationship with God, the soul is best understood as the *self* or *person* to whom that image and capacity has been given. As the Second Helvetic Confession states:

> Now concerning man, Scripture says that in the beginning he was made good according to the image and likeness of God. . . . We also affirm that man consists of two different substances in one person: an immortal soul which, when separated from the body, neither sleeps nor dies, and a mortal body which will nevertheless be raised up from the dead at the last judgment, in order that then the whole man, either in life or in death, abide forever.[11]

The Westminster Confession of Faith elaborates on this understanding of the soul:

After God had made all other creatures, he created man, male and female, with reasonable and immortal souls, endued with knowledge, righteousness, and true holiness after his own image, having the law of God written in their hearts, and power to fulfill it; and yet under a possibility of transgressing, being left to the liberty of their own will, which was subject unto change. Besides this law written in their hearts, they received a command not to eat of the tree of the knowledge of good and evil; which while they kept they were happy in their communion with God, and had dominion over the creatures.[12]

This language is admittedly dualistic.[13] It distinguishes the soul and the body as two distinct substances, the body being material, the soul being immaterial.[14] Modern scholarship insists that the biblical view of humanity is not so dualistic.

Yet this confessional language is important. It insists on the reality of the soul. This soul, like the body, is creaturely, finite, and dependent. But the self cannot be reduced to a function of the body. Rather, the soul or self expresses itself through the body. As John Leith notes, "Materialists of one kind or another think of the self or the mind as a function of the brain. Yet there is good reason to insist that the self uses the brain as its instrument."[15] While the nature of the soul may remain mysterious, and its relation to the body hard to define or explicate, surely no one who is self-conscious can doubt the existence of the self.

Discussion of the image of God and the soul leads to discussion of free will and its misuse in sin. The most helpful discussion of the freedom of the will as an aspect of the human soul (and as part of the image of God in humanity) appears in the Westminster Confession of Faith.[16]

Westminster sets forth four distinct stages of human freedom. First, human beings are created free and able to sin or not to sin. Second, having exercised the freedom to sin, human beings have fallen into a situation of bondage to sin, of not being able not to sin. We are not free to return to God on our own.

Third, when God takes the initiative to convert someone and bring him or her into a state of grace, there is a new and partial freedom in being able not to sin. We are able freely to will and to do that which is spiritually good, though never without the continuing taint of self-interest. As I like to say, on a good day, in small and fragmentary ways, we are able to do something which is not totally sinful.

Fourth and finally, only in the life to come is a human being raised to a condition of not being able to sin. Ironically, while this condition may sound like a loss of freedom of choice, it is actually the highest freedom of all. Sin is no longer even a possibility.

The Doctrine of Sin

It is significant that the church's early confessions address sin in the context of the remission and forgiveness of sin.[17] Sin is the occasion for forgiveness, the negative presumption of salvation. Sin is not so much a subject in its own right as that from which God extricates humanity in order to restore humanity to a right relationship with God.

The doctrine of original sin is of particular concern in a consideration of human nature. This doctrine refers to humanity's first sin, Adam and Eve's disobedience, which is understood to have infected not only them but human nature itself and therefore *all* individual humans. The Scots Confession states:

> By this transgression, generally known as original sin, the image of God was utterly defaced in man, and he and his children became by nature hostile to God, slaves to Satan, and servants to sin. And thus everlasting death has had, and shall have, power and dominion over all who have not been, are not, or shall not be reborn from above.[18]

It is from this "corrupt nature" that actual and specific sins flow.[19] Thus, the Second Helvetic Confession says:

> By sin we understand that innate corruption of man which has been derived or propagated in us all from our first parents, by which we, immersed in perverse desires and averse to all good, are included [*sic;* read "inclined"] to all evil. Full of all wickedness, distrust, contempt and hatred of God, we are unable to do or even to think anything good of ourselves. Moreover, even as we grow older, so by wicked thoughts, words,

and deeds committed against God's law, we bring forth corrupt fruit worthy of an evil tree.[20]

The doctrine of original sin raises particular problems for contemporary understandings of human nature. First, philosophical views of reality have changed from the time of the Reformation. Some would question whether there is any such thing as abstract human nature, independent from specific human individuals, to be affected by original sin.[21] Nonetheless, the doctrine of original sin articulates what should be obvious, namely, that all human beings have turned away from God.

Second, several Reformed confessions state clearly that original sin is passed on through natural or ordinary generation (that is, conception).[22] If it were the case that original sin is part of our biological inheritance, we should be able to find a bad gene or genes responsible for sin, and with the advent of genetic engineering we should be able to correct or eliminate it. But the doctrine of original sin points to something much more complex. Original sin is not a bodily ailment, but a disorienting and maiming affliction of the soul, or the self.

The human person is a great mystery. We do not yet and may well never understand the connection between biological conception and the creation of a human soul. What we do know is that all human selves, created to be focused and centered upon God, have become focused and centered upon themselves. We cannot save ourselves from this malady. Indeed, our very efforts to save ourselves are further expressions of the self-interest from which we seek and need to be saved. This self-centeredness is the fundamental human problem. Individual sins, while a consequence of this condition, are distinct from it. Attempts by genetic engineering to modify or eliminate "sinful" behaviors, whether successful or not, cannot eliminate this condition.

Finally, because sin has effaced the image of God in human nature, we can no longer tell what is truly human simply by looking at human beings. Rather, because Jesus Christ is truly human yet without sin, we discern true human being in him. As the Westminster Confession of Faith states:

> The Son of God, the second Person in the Trinity, being very and eternal God, of one substance, and equal with the

Father, did, when the fullness of time was come, take upon
him man's nature, with all the essential properties and common infirmities thereof; yet without sin: being conceived by
the power of the Holy Ghost, in the womb of the Virgin
Mary, of her substance. So that two whole, perfect, and distinct natures, the Godhead and the manhood, were insepa-
rably joined together in one person, without conversion,
composition, or confusion. Which person is very God and
very man, yet one Christ, the only Mediator between God
and man.[23]

Thus, while Adam and Eve were disobedient, Jesus Christ was
obedient; while we are self-centered, he is God-centered; while we
are hurtful of each other, he accepted self-sacrifice; while we are sinful, he is innocent and holy. As the Confession of 1967 says:

In Jesus of Nazareth, true humanity was realized once for all.
Jesus, a Palestinian Jew, lived among his own people and
shared their needs, temptations, joys, and sorrows. He expressed the love of God in word and deed and became a
brother to all kinds of sinful men. But his complete obedi-
ence led him into conflict with his people. His life and teaching judged their goodness, religious aspirations, and national
hopes. Many rejected him and demanded his death. In giving himself freely for them, he took upon himself the judgment under which all men stand convicted. God raised him
from the dead, vindicating him as Messiah and Lord. The victim of sin became victor, and won the victory over sin and
death for all men.[24]

In Jesus Christ, we see true humanity as God meant it to be.
While biology points toward our relatedness to all life (so that some
are reluctant to speak of any special creation of humanity), the incarnation of Christ clearly establishes (or we might say reestablishes) our
special and unique relationship with God.[25]

Conclusions

This brief survey of the historical Reformed doctrines of human nature, the soul, and sin has several implications for current discussions

of genetic engineering. First, in that human beings are created and finite, they face certain insurmountable givens, such as differences in
strength, intelligence, and capability. This God-given diversity is at
least partially based in genetic diversity. It cannot simply be undone
by religious wishfulness, government decree, or political correctness.

While advanced technology may be able to ameliorate some of
the factors (such as disease) that disadvantage some humans, reducing biological diversity may create new problems.[26] In any case, none
of us can escape the reality of death. No matter how much disease is
reduced, no matter how long life is extended, death will not be erad-
icated. War, crime, infectious disease, starvation, and suicide will continue to remind us of our finitude.

Second, in that human beings are created in the image of God
(that is, with a soul, or self, that is self-conscious and capable of tran-
scendence), Christians can welcome and appreciate the sciences'
quest for knowledge and benefits to humanity. Christians have no
need to fear the truth, since we regard God as the author and source
of all truth. The Reformed tradition has been especially committed to
the service of God through the life of the mind. Reformed Christians
have seen the teachings of John Calvin to be supportive of science,
industry, technology, and capitalism.

At the same time, Christians should not fear to speak the truth of
the gospel. Human pretensions can become idolatrous. Such idolatry
can occur in the political realm or in religion itself. It can also occur
in science. The general public does not always appreciate that the sciences are thoroughly human endeavors. While they have proven
themselves delightfully brilliant and fruitful in human efforts to understand and manipulate the world in all its complexity, the sciences
are also finite, flawed, and laden with human values, motives, and in-
terests, like every other human endeavor. Christians will be wary of
claims made in the name of science that fail to acknowledge these
limitations. The Reformed tradition has been particularly critical of
utopian claims.

Third, in that human beings are sinful and self-interested, we will
be critically aware that every advance in knowledge and technique,
every new achievement, every new opportunity for good, carries with
it the possibility—indeed, the likelihood—that we will misuse and
pervert it. We need not avoid these efforts to advance, despite the

dangers. But we must be diligent, self-critical, and never surprised by the presence, strength, deep-rootedness, or tenacity of evil.

Fourth and finally, in that human beings are not only finite (by virtue of being created), transcendent (by virtue of being created in the image of God), and fallen (by virtue of sin), but also redeemed (by virtue of Jesus Christ), Christians are able to live in gratitude for the gift of life but also in the realization that this life is not ultimate. No matter how much life might be genetically enhanced or how long it might be extended, this effort to give "new" life does not approach and does not have anything to do with what the church has called the resurrection and eternal life. We are only passing through here on our long journey home to God.

NOTES

1. Those churches most closely associated with the theology of the Reformer John Calvin (1509–1564) have been called Reformed, insofar as they have expressed their intent to reform their life more thoroughly according to the Word of God. Change is not for the sake of change, but for the sake of greater faithfulness to God.

This chapter draws in particular on the official confessions of faith of the Presbyterian Church (U.S.A.): the Nicene Creed (hereafter abbreviated as NC), the Apostles' Creed (AC), the Scots Confession (SC), the Heidelberg Catechism (HC), the Second Helvetic Confession (SHC), the Westminster Confession of Faith (WCF), the Larger Catechism (WLC), the Shorter Catechism (WSC), the Theological Declaration of Barmen (TDB), the Confession of 1967 (C67), and A Brief Statement of Faith—Presbyterian Church (U.S.A.) (BSF). See *Book of Confessions* (Louisville, Ky.: Office of the General Assembly [Presbyterian Church (U.S.A.)], 1996).

2. *Book of Order* (Louisville, Ky.: Office of the General Assembly [Presbyterian Church (U.S.A.)], 1995), G-2.0100.

3. WSC 7.001 (p. 181); see also WLC 7.111 (p. 201).

4. NC 1.1 (p. 3).

5. AC 2.1 (p. 7), SC 3.01 (p. 11), HC 4.001 (p. 29), SHC 5.032 (p. 63), WCF 6.022 (p. 130), WSC 7.009 (p. 181), WLC 7.125 (pp. 202–203), C67 9.16 (p. 263), and BSF 10.3 (line 29, p. 275).

6. While some biologists do regard human life as a chance occurrence, it is worth noting that evolutionary biological theory attempts to account for the origin and differentiation of species, not for the origin of

life itself. In a similar way, the Big Bang theory attempts to account for the unimaginably rapid expansion of matter, space, and even time from an infinitesimal point, but it cannot, and does not pretend to, account for the origin of that point itself.

7. HC 4.001 (p. 29), 4.026 (p. 32), 4.027 (p. 33), and 4.028 (p. 33).

8. WSC 7.004 (p. 181); see also WCF 6.011 (p. 128) and WLC 7.117 (pp. 201–202).

9. SC 3.02 (p. 11).

10. HC 4.006 (p. 30); see also C67 9.17 (p. 263), and BSF 10.3 (lines 29–32, p. 275).

11. SHC 5.034 (p. 64).

12. WCF 6.023 (p. 130); see also WSC 7.010 (p. 181), WLC 7.127 (p. 203), and C67 9.17 (p. 263).

13. See also SC 3.17 (p. 19), HC 4.057 (p. 37), SHC 5.034 (p. 64), WCF 6.023 (p. 130), and WCF 6.177 (p. 163).

14. Some who deny this dualism hold to another "dualism," that is, that God and the world are distinct. Others deny both kinds of dualism.

15. John H. Leith, *Basic Christian Doctrine* (Louisville, Ky.: Westminster John Knox, 1993), 112.

16. WCF 6.059-63 (pp. 137–138); see also SHC 5.043 (p. 66).

17. NC 1.3 (p. 3) and AC 2.3 (p. 7).

18. SC 3.03 (pp. 11–12); see also HC 4.007 (p. 30), WCF 6.031–33 (p. 132), WSC 7.014–16 (p. 182), WLC 7.131–136 (pp. 203–204). For the development of the doctrine of sin in Reformed theology, see Heinrich Heppe, *Reformed Dogmatics: Set Out and Illustrated from the Sources,* foreword by Karl Barth, rev. and ed. Ernst Bizer, trans. G. T. Thomson (Grand Rapids, Mich.: Baker Book House, 1978), Chapter XV, "Sin, or Man's State of Corruption and Misery," 320–370.

19. SC 3.13 (pp. 16–17).

20. SHC 5.037 (pp. 64–65); see also WCF 6.034–36 (p. 132), WSC 7.017–19 (p. 182), WLC 7.133–39 (p. 204), C67 9.12 (p. 263), BSF 10.3 (lines 33–38, p. 275).

21. Compare I. Lehr Brisbin and Ronald Cole-Turner in chapters 5 and 8 of this book. Their understanding of evolutionary history would preclude a special creation of humanity, a historical fall, and thus original sin.

22. HC 4.07 (p. 30), SHC 5.036–37 (pp. 64–65), WCF 6.033 (p. 132), WSC 7.016 (p. 182), and WLC 7.136 (p. 204); see also SC 3.03 (pp. 11–12).

23. WCF 6.044 (pp. 133–34); see also NC 1.2 (p. 3), AC 2.2 (p. 7), SC 3.06 (p. 13), HC 4.015 (p. 31), HC 4.035 (p. 34), WSC 7.022 (p. 183), WLC 7.147 (p. 206), and BSF 10.2 (p. 275).

24. C67 9.08 (p. 262).

25. Evolutionary biologists have noted that human genes include many pre-human genes. In this sense, Christ assumed humanity specifically but not exclusively. Christ redeems the whole creation.

26. See I. Lehr Brisbin and Ronald Cole-Turner in chapters 5 and 8 of this book.

Summary

The church's confessions remind us that we are created to be in relationship with God. Yet we have misused our freedom and have turned away from God. We depend on God's grace in Jesus Christ to restore us.

This basic story of creation, sin, and salvation has implications for our understanding of science. Even the greatest achievements of science cannot alter our basic condition: we are finite, limited, and diverse. We can seek the truths that science teaches, yet we are also aware of our capacity to misuse science. Finally, our lives belong ultimately to God. We are to trust in God alone, and to live grateful lives in response to God's gift of salvation in Christ.

Study Questions

1. How is the Reformed doctrine of humanity different from or similar to an evolutionary view of human origins?
2. What, according to the confessions, is the purpose of human life?
3. What does it mean to be created in the image of God?
4. What is the soul?
5. Why can we not overcome sin ourselves?
6. When does the Christian faith have reason to criticize the claims of science?

Chapter 8

Human Nature as Seen by Science and Faith

Ronald Cole-Turner

Faithful Response to Science

Can I be a Christian and still look at the world through the eyes of science? Can I see myself as created in God's image and saved by Christ's grace, and *also* as a biological organism, a product of a long evolutionary process? Must I choose between faith and science, or can I have both?

Many today say no: faith and science are incompatible, especially on topics like evolution and human nature. Some scientists, for example, insist that evolution contradicts creation. Evolution is by chance, creation by design. According to evolution, they say, we are animals without souls, a view at odds with the Bible. Many Christians agree, and they choose their faith over the findings of science.

But is it really true that science and faith conflict, or that evolution and creation are incompatible? Do we really have to choose between seeing ourselves as God's creatures or as evolved organisms?

Darwin's *The Origin of Species* had scarcely appeared when Christians stepped forward with the idea that evolution, far from contradicting Christianity, made it more plausible and relevant.[1] Gregor Mendel, who discovered the fundamental principles of genetics, was a monk who pursued his work as part of his religious devotion. Early in this century, as biologists brought the ideas of Darwin and Mendel together, many theologians used the new biology to expound a new Christian view of human nature.

In the 1920s and '30s, however, evolution and genetics became linked with coercive eugenics programs, first in the United States, then in Nazi Germany. Quite rightly, some church leaders protested clearly and strongly that the church's theology of humanity must be based on God's revelation in Christ, not on notions of humanity that come from science or a human ideology.

Today, we face a new challenge. Genetics and neuroscience offer us rich and compelling ways to understand all living things, including ourselves, as kindred beings linked in a vast evolutionary and ecological web of life. Technical advances make it possible for us to alter the genetic code and other fundamental biological processes. We stand at the threshold of a new era in human self-understanding and human self-alteration.

Our theology of human nature must remain grounded in God's revelation in Christ. At the same time, new questions have now come to the fore: How in the growing light of science do we unfold the truth of this revelation? How do we understand our thoughts and behaviors, and our responsibility for them, in light of the role that our genes and our brain play in determining who we are? And, more urgently, how does our faith in Jesus Christ lead us to respond to the growing power of technology to alter our human nature?

Science does challenge our faith, but as a resource, not a threat. We are poised at the beginning of what may be a new and enriched era of Christian thinking. Unparalleled advances in science now make it possible for us to work for corresponding advances in our Christian understanding of the biological creation and human nature. As never before, we can begin to use scientific research as an aid in answering the perennial religious question, "Who are we?"

And we must not delay, for already we have to ask, "What should we make of ourselves?" Our biological nature will soon be subject to biotechnological revision. The church needs to be prepared to share the burden of deciding how we will use this power. But we will be ready only when we have developed an understanding of human nature that is based on the best theological and scientific thinking available.

Human Nature: Traditional Theological Views

According to traditional Christian theology, human beings are like other animals: we are made of the dust of the ground. But we are unlike all other animals in several important ways. Our mental capacities are far greater, our emotional sensitivities far more subtle, and our social relationships far richer and more complex than those of any other species. We alone have the capacity for spoken language, for moral awareness, for free moral choice, for creativity, and, perhaps most importantly, for a relationship with God, a relationship that we believe will continue forever. These special capacities, taken together, are the human soul.[2]

For many theologians, the soul is fundamentally distinct from the body, even to the point of being a separate substance, a different kind of being than the physical body. From this perspective, the soul is able to survive the body at death or even to leave the body temporarily during dreams or moments of ecstasy.

At the same time, most Christian theologians have avoided philosophical dualism, which distinguishes so sharply between body and soul that the body is seen as inferior, even intrinsically dirty or evil, and best left behind. "Absolutely not!" the theologians of the church insist. God made the human body good. In Christ, God is incarnate in a body just like ours. And most importantly, Christ died and rose again so that our bodies, too, may be raised to life forever with God. In raising the body, God transforms it so that this changed body, with its extraordinary capabilities or soul, can enjoy the presence of God forever.

According to the Christian tradition, however, it is naively optimistic for us to focus only on our human capacities. These gifts have been twisted and tarnished. Yes, we have a sense of moral obligation, but we often disregard it. We have rich and complex relationships with others, but so often we betray or destroy them. We have a capacity for a relationship with God, but we tend to hide from God and live as if God had no claim on us. Traditional theology has attributed this situation to original sin. God made us good in every respect, but in Adam and Eve we chose moral disorder and alienation from God. We are so incapacitated that, without God's grace in Christ, we cannot save ourselves or reestablish a right relationship with God.

The Challenge for Theology Today

This traditional theology of human nature is strongly challenged by recent science, according to which there are no Adam and Eve, no Fall, no sharp distinction between ourselves and other animals, and no soul as a separate substance. These are all serious differences. We cannot ignore them. We cannot simply say: evolution is about the body, theology is about the soul, and so nothing about evolution challenges our theology. Evolution *is* about the soul. Evolution is an explanation of how the human species, with all our capacities, became distinct from other species. Especially as it is understood today in light of genetics and neuroscience, evolution is about how our capacities (that is, the human soul) came into existence, how they are structured, and how they are limited.

The challenge to Christian theology today is immense. According to the theory of evolution, all species come into existence through the interaction of random genetic mutations and natural selection. Human beings share this evolutionary origin with bacteria, insects, birds, and reptiles, as well as with other mammals, to which we are most closely linked in our evolutionary history.

We are also challenged by findings that relate us to other human-like creatures.[3] Modern human beings have undergone only slight evolution in the last 50,000 to 100,000 years. For part of that time, our ancestors lived side by side with other hominids who were very much like us, usually known as Neanderthals. These Neanderthals were not brutes, as sometimes thought, but made and used sophisticated tools and had complex, possibly caring societies, probably grieving at a time of death and perhaps wondering about life after death.

Evolutionary theory lifts up several key tensions. One is the tension between inheritance and environment. Like Neanderthals and other primates, we human beings are the product of evolution. We bear its legacy in our genes. Indeed, some of our genes are truly ancient. And with only small differences, we share many of our genes with other species.

At the same time, our gifts and capacities, together with their limits, are the result of the *interaction* between the genes that we inherit and the environment that envelopes us. At conception, genes provide instructions that guide the fertilized egg in its divisions from one cell into many, and then in the specialization of cells into the various tissues and organs that make up our bodies. At each stage, the genetic instructions interact with the environment, both physical and social/cultural.

A second tension is between individuality and commonality. Each human being is unique. Even so-called identical twins, who come from the same fertilized egg and thus are substantially alike genetically, have different life histories and different environments. Our capacities and our limits are uniquely our own.

But we also share many things with other human beings. Language is found in every culture, as is a capacity for community, art, and humor, along with an awareness of death and even a sense of a mysterious or holy dimension in what surrounds us. Humans seem to share the same weaknesses, anxieties, hostilities toward strangers, and abilities to betray friends and family.

A third tension is between determination and freedom. On the one hand, we are not born as neutral or blank slates. Evolution has given us certain capacities that we inherit in our genes. Each of us is a unique mix of a common evolutionary history. Our capacities are uniquely structured, conditioned, and limited. Through behavior genetics and neuroscience, we are discovering, for example, the role that neurotransmitters play in the processes of the brain. Unusual levels of neurotransmitters such as dopamine or serotonin seem to trigger depression and may also account for aggressive behavior and a tendency toward addiction to alcohol or other substances. These neurotransmitter levels are the result of genetic and environmental factors, acting together.

Moreover, evolution has also given us a capacity for morality and religion. We seem to inherit a sense of right and wrong and even of the sacred or holy, which we then express in ways that are uniquely our own. We also appear to inherit a unique, individual set of propensities that incline us toward certain patterns of behavior and away from others, or toward particular traits of personality and away from others.

On the other hand, we seem to be able to choose specific deeds or attitudes freely, despite these propensities or inclinations. As research in behavior genetics advances, we might learn that some individuals inherit a genetic predisposition toward a certain class of addictive drugs. Nevertheless, most of us (including the police and the courts!) will continue to believe that virtually everyone is sufficiently free to be morally responsible for the use of drugs, and so morally and criminally liable for bad choices.

No doubt we will find it increasingly tempting to blame our behavior on our genes. Blaming genes for our bad choices, however, is simply not supported by genetics research. Marital infidelity, bigotry, and drug abuse may all have some basis in our genes, but blaming our moral failure on our genes is not science. It is excuse-making. Our genes may help explain who we are, but they do not excuse what we do.

Theology, Science, and Human Nature

This notion that we are conditioned yet free, or genetically inclined toward a certain behavior yet free to choose or resist, is remarkably similar to the Christian theological view of our human nature as richly gifted yet fallen. Even in our fallenness, theologians insist, we are free to choose or to resist. We and we alone—not our environment or our genetic inheritance—are responsible. When we sin, we are without excuse, even if we have very good explanations.

Indeed, the view emerging from the sciences is especially similar to that developed by John Calvin and the great theologians of the Reformed tradition, who believed that our natural gifts are distorted: we are inclined to ignore God and forsake our obligations. But when we do so, they insisted, each of us alone is to blame, not our environment or even our fallen nature. It is true, they would say, that the story of the Fall of Adam and Eve explains why we inherit a disordered moral and spiritual nature. But it does not excuse our sins. Sin has no excuse. We are, as they insisted again and again, always "without excuse."

In place of the story of Adam and Eve, Christian theology today can turn to evolution and genetics to explain our origin, nature, and ambiguous moral and spiritual condition. When we ask theologically about human nature in light of evolution, the fundamental picture remains the same: we possess rich gifts, but we consistently fail to live as God intends.

Nevertheless, there are important differences between traditional theology and contemporary science. When we open ourselves to the insights of science, our theological views will be affected. Indeed, science cannot enrich our theology if we are closed to that possibility.

What happens then when we draw evolution and genetics into a theological understanding of human nature? What revisions are we led to make? First, we see that we human beings are not as different from other species as we once thought. The differences between us and other primates, like chimpanzees, are small when compared to the difference between a dog and a cat. Those small genetic differences that distinguish us from the chimpanzees obviously give us several capacities that far exceed what chimps can do. Nevertheless, all life is on a continuum or unbroken spectrum, sharing fundamental processes even while differing in important respects. We are not the result of a special act of creation. We are just one small part of the rich diversity of life on earth, far more dependent on this diversity than we realized before.

Second, genetics asks us to revise our theology of human nature by recognizing more profoundly the differences between individual human beings. As individuals, we are a unique collection of genes. To the extent that our capacities are conditioned by our genes, we inherit unique capacities. Moreover, we inherit unique predispositions or tendencies; we are inclined uniquely and individually to a complex set of behaviors or traits. What appeals to one of us may repel another, and what tempts one may not entice another. The strength of temptation for any particular sin varies from person to person. One of us may find the temptation to misuse alcohol to be a nearly insurmountable problem, while others are not tempted.

We therefore need, third, to revise our understanding of the freedom of the will, especially the strength of the will to resist a specific impulse, or the weakness of the will in the face of a particular evil. The human will is an evolved capacity. It is formed and structured by our genes as they interact with the environment. It is only as strong as the neural processes that sustain it. The shape and the strength of these processes vary, person to person.

There is no abstract or disembodied human free will. If there were, we would all have the same strength in resisting each temptation or in meeting each moral or spiritual challenge, regardless of our genes or our environment. But our wills—their structure, their strength, their complex impulses and desires—are uniquely our own, for they are formed by our unique genes and our unique environment. Because our moral and spiritual capacities will differ, as will our inclinations toward various sins, we need to see ourselves as tempted in various ways.

In sum, we all live in the same world, and we all face the same attractions, enticingly displayed in the supermarket of good and bad possibilities that surround us. And we are all confronted by the moral and spiritual challenge of living a faithful Christian life. Our will is not absolutely free and neutral. Rather, it is inclined in various ways and limited in its capacities to choose.

Traditional theology accepted the idea that we are subject to such inner inclinations and even that we inherit these inclinations through biological processes. What is new here is that genetics shows us that we are individually and variously inclined, each in our own way. In the decades ahead, we should expect that genetics will further explain the relationships between the genes that we inherit and the patterns of behavior that we exhibit. As we learn these things about ourselves and about others, we will have growing reason to be patient and compassionate with each other when we fail morally and spiritually.

The Technological Alteration of Human Nature

Should we use genetics and neuroscience to alter our human nature? Should we alter the processes of our brains, so that our very soul is affected? Overwhelming as they are, these questions are already upon us, and the church should participate in their public discussion.

Christians have always been in favor of alteration and improvement of our moral and spiritual capacities. We have used various methods, such as preaching, teaching, counseling, prayer, memorization, and fasting, to improve ourselves and others morally and spiritually. While the Spirit alone is able to work the inner transformation of the self, we have been convinced that the Spirit works through preachers and teachers and other external means of grace.

We have sometimes used the most dramatic terms imaginable to describe religious transformation: being "born again," "regeneration," becoming a "new creation," and putting off the "old self" in order to be made new in Christ. Indeed, the gospel is all about human transformation, a fundamental redefinition of our personal identity, as symbolized through our baptism. Christians believe that we are unable to begin this process on our own; only the unilateral initiative or grace of God makes it possible. Through grace, God heals our very self. Our lives become more coherent, more focused on that which is good, and more capable morally and spiritually.

In thinking about this transformation process, we need to avoid a dualism that says: Christ changes the soul but not the body. Yes, of course, the grace of God in Jesus Christ changes the structure and the condition of our soul. As we are put into right relationship with God, we are transformed so that we begin to think and act differently. But this transformation is a change of the soul-and-body, a change that affects the brain and the ways in which it functions.

Once it was thought that the human brain was essentially hardwired at birth, and that little change occurred, especially after adolescence. Now we are learning that the brain changes and adapts to new situations (and responds badly to protracted stress from experiences such as combat or sexual abuse, possibly in ways that result in irreversible loss to brain functions).[4] At this stage in scientific research, we are unable to say how our encounter with God's grace brings about specific neurological changes. But this much is clear: unless the brain itself is altered, we (that is, the center of our self, our person, or our soul) are not really changed.

In the future, we should expect neuroscience to explore, with increasing interest, how prayer, meditation, or religious ritual alters our brain activity and makes it possible for us to come to a more profound sense of the transcendent. The pervasive spiritual hunger of our age, coupled with our impatience, may lead before long to efforts to use technological interventions to induce spiritual states. Indeed, some have already advocated the use of hallucinogenic drugs for just this purpose.

Most of us take the warnings about such drugs seriously and stay away from them. But if newer, safer, more moderate and reliable techniques were available, more of us might try this alternate route to spiritual awareness.

We already see widespread use of antidepressants, such as Prozac. These drugs alter neurotransmitter activity. In ways that no one yet understands, they assist significantly not only in relieving depression or anxiety, but also in giving people a greater sense of focus, productivity, and confidence.[5] We have reason to fear that some people now ask for these drugs not because they are depressed, but because they want to be at peak performance, so that they can compete successfully with others who use these drugs. They believe that these drugs give them a boost that they cannot attain otherwise.

As we learn more in the not-too-distant future about the role that genes play in the structuring of our brains, we will find new ways to alter human nature, including that of future generations. Many of us are deeply disturbed by this prospect, even if we are not quite able to say why. We take comfort in the thought that the genetics of complex capacities, such as intelligence, may never be well-understood.

Even so, some will be tempted to believe that "scientists" can manipulate the genes of our offspring to boost intelligence, gregariousness, or other traits that give one an advantage in a competitive society. Those who can afford such experiments will of course be those who already enjoy a financial advantage. We would then have to ask: Would our unaltered children be forced to live with a competitive disadvantage?

More realistically, we may learn the location of genes that lead to certain predispositions or mental illnesses. If so, people may want to have pregnancies tested prenatally and perhaps aborted if they do not like what they find. Should there be government constraints on what we can do? Should there be pressure to test fetuses and terminate pregnancies in order to avoid costly mental health care?

And if we alter our children so that they do not inherit a particular predisposition, will we have relieved them, even in the smallest way, of what traditional theology calls original sin? If our genes structure and even compromise our will, should we turn to genetic interventions for a therapy for our sinful nature? Would genetics then displace the grace of God in the process of human transformation? If genetics can eliminate any of the morally or spiritually distressing aspects of evolution and make our offspring more focused and capable as spiritual and moral agents, should we rush to embrace it, seeing it as our way of participating in God's work, or is it the ultimate defiance of our Creator and Redeemer?

Drugs like Prozac already pose some of these questions, and the answers are not yet clear. On the one hand, such drugs may cause us to think that we do not need grace or further change. On the other, they may cause us to recognize, perhaps clearly for the first time, that only a transforming grace can bring us into right relationship with God.

The question of genetic alteration of our offspring will engulf the church as we make our way into the next century. Most often, it will be framed as a medical or a legal debate. The church, however, must insist that it is, above all, a religious debate, a debate about the transformation of the human body-and-soul, the human self. But if we are to be heard in the public debate, we need to be prepared theologically so that we may participate credibly and effectively. Our theology needs to be as sophisticated as the technology it addresses.

The human experiment has only begun. As never before, we need a courageous church filled with people who see the world through both science and faith. For if the church chooses faith but not science, the world will no doubt choose science but not faith. And then we all will have chosen to reject the claims of the God who patiently awaited our arrival on this planet and who even now invites us to be made new in Jesus Christ.

NOTES

1. See David N. Livingstone, *Darwin's Forgotten Defenders: The Encounter between Evangelical Theology and Evolutionary Thought* (Grand Rapids, Mich.: Eerdmans, 1987); and James R. Moore, *The Post-Darwinian Controversies: A Study of the Protestant Struggle to Come to Terms with Darwin in Great Britain and America, 1870–1900* (Cambridge: Cambridge University Press, 1979).

2. By defining the human soul as a set of capacities, I am departing from the view that it is a separate substance or, as is commonly thought today, that it is self-consciousness, such as suggested by James Goodloe in chapter 7 of this book. Like Karl Barth, I believe that theology in the past has made too much of the soul. Barth "remained unconvinced that the question of the so-called 'soul' ought to dominate this sphere of dogmatics [that is, theological anthropology] so fully as was the case in the

older theologians." See Karl Barth, *Church Dogmatics III/2, The Doctrine of Creation,* trans. Harold Knight, G. W. Bromiley, J. K. S. Reid, and R. H. Fuller (Edinburgh: T. & T. Clark, 1960), ix.

3. In February 1997, *National Geographic* began a series, "The Dawn of Humans," which summarizes recent scientific discoveries in human evolution.

4. For a review of recent studies, see Robert M. Sapolsky, "Why Stress is Bad for Your Brain," *Science* 273 (August 9, 1997): 749–750.

5. Peter D. Kramer, *Listening to Prozac: A Psychiatrist Explores Antidepressant Drugs and the Remaking of the Self* (New York: Viking, 1993); and Simon Barondes, "Thinking about Prozac," *Science* 263 (February 25, 1994): 1102–1103.

Summary

Evolutionary theory poses a profound challenge to traditional theological formulations about human nature. We now see ourselves as having an evolutionary origin, like all other creatures. Our soul—our capacity for language, moral responsibility, and relationship with God—as much as our body is a product of genetic mutation and natural selection.

Evolution and genetics describe humans in terms of several key tensions. First, we are shaped by our genetic inheritance, yet in interaction with our environment. Second, we are unique individuals, yet also share much in common with other humans. Third, our genes and environment predispose and limit us, yet we also make choices within those constraints. Thus, our freedom is always conditioned; it is never absolute.

Some of the most difficult questions have to do with our growing ability to alter the genetic base of these conditions. These genetic alterations can affect not only our physical but also our mental and spiritual state. The church's theology—which also stresses that we are free, yet limited (by finitude and sin)—might help us to respond to these developments.

Study Questions

1. What are some of the ways in which evolutionary theory challenges traditional Christian understandings of creation and sin?
2. How do traditional Christian theology and contemporary genetic research speak to the question of freedom versus determination?
3. How could the insights of genetic research assist us in ministering to people who fail morally or spiritually?
4. What issues does the genetic alteration of humans raise? What kinds of alterations are permissible, and what are not?
5. What do you think of the idea that certain genetic alterations might give us a deeper sense of God's presence and grace?

Questions for Further Reflection

1. What does it mean to be created "in the image of God"? How are humans like animals? How are they not like animals? How are humans like God? How are they not like God? Has God given humans unique abilities and responsibilities?

2. Is there any room left for the notion of a soul, in light of contemporary science? To what degree are we simply the product of evolutionary forces? How might the apostle Paul's assertion that we are part of a new creation in Christ (2 Corinthians 5:17) affect the way we think about these questions?

3. How does genetic research change our understanding of the forces that determine, condition, and limit us? Is it still possible to talk about human freedom? Does this research suggest that we are more free or less free than we imagined?

4. How does genetic research change our understanding of human relationships? To what degree is everybody really the same "under the skin"? To what degree are our differences greater than we once thought? Does genetic research confirm or call into question the Christian hope of love and unity?

5. What constitutes human wholeness? What can we learn from genetic research about human wholeness? To what degree can we

ourselves help to bring human wholeness about? To what degree must we receive it as a gift of God?

6. What kinds of attitudes do Christians express about science? What kinds of attitudes do scientists express about religion in general and Christianity in particular? What are some current examples of conflict between some religious people and some scientists? At what points can science contribute to a deeper sense of wonder at, and worship of, God? At what points do people make claims in the name of science ... Christians must question? What could the church be doing to help people in religious and scientific communities to understand each other better?

Suggestions for Further Reading

While literature on the new genetics is growing rapidly, several books are especially helpful to a broad church audience. For a basic introduction to the Human Genome Project, the science behind it, and ethical, legal, and social issues raised by the project, see Catherine Baker, *Your Genes, Your Choices: Exploring the Issues Raised by Genetic Research* (Washington, D.C.: American Association for the Advancement of Science, 1997).

For insightful reflections on recent developments in genetic research and their theological and ethical implications, see Ronald Cole-Turner, ed., *Human Cloning: Religious Responses* (Louisville, Ky.: Westminster John Knox, 1997); Ronald Cole-Turner, *The New Genesis: Theology and the Genetic Revolution* (Louisville, Ky.: Westminster John Knox, 1993); and Ronald Cole-Turner and Brent Waters, *Pastoral Genetics: Theology and Care at the Beginning of Life* (Louisville, Ky.: Westminster John Knox, 1996).

Other volumes that helpfully explore these issues are John F. Kilner, Rebecca D. Pentz, and Frank E. Young, eds., *Genetic Ethics: Do the Ends Justify the Genes?* (Grand Rapids, Mich.: Eerdmans, 1997); and Gerald P. McKenny, *To Relieve the Human Condition: Bioethics, Technology, and the Body* (Albany, N.Y.: SUNY Press, 1997).

For an introduction to classic Christian (and especially Reformed) perspectives on human nature, see John H. Leith, *Basic Christian Doctrine* (Louisville, Ky.: Westminster John Knox, 1993); and John H. Leith, *Introduction to the Reformed Tradition: A Way of Being the Christian Community,* rev. ed. (Atlanta: John Knox, 1977, 1981). A useful introduction to the confessions of the Presbyterian Church (U.S.A.) and their major themes is Jack Rogers, *Presbyterian Creeds: A Guide to The Book of Confessions,* rev. ed. (Louisville, Ky.: Westminster John Knox, 1992).

Major theologians in this century have reflected extensively on the nature of humanity before God. Two demanding but significant works from recent decades are Jürgen Moltmann, *Man: Christian Anthropology in the Conflicts of the Present* (Philadelphia: Fortress Press, 1974); and Wolfhart Pannenberg, *Anthropology in Theological Perspective* (Philadelphia: Westminster, 1985).

Contributors

James Ayers is Pastor of the South Frankfort Presbyterian Church in Frankfort, Kentucky.

I. Lehr Brisbin, Jr., is a Senior Research Ecologist at the University of Georgia's Savannah River Ecology Laboratory in Aiken, South Carolina.

John P. Burgess is Associate for Theology in the Office of Theology and Worship (Christian Faith and Life Area, Congregational Ministries Division) of the Presbyterian Church (U.S.A.) in Louisville, Kentucky. In 1998, he will become Associate Professor of Theology at Pittsburgh Theological Seminary in Pittsburgh, Pennsylvania.

R. David Cole is Professor Emeritus of Molecular and Cell Biology at the University of California in Berkeley, California.

Ronald Cole-Turner is Associate Professor of Theology and Ethics at Pittsburgh Theological Seminary in Pittsburgh, Pennsylvania.

James C. Goodloe IV is Pastor of the Grace Covenant Presbyterian Church in Richmond, Virginia.

James B. Miller is Senior Program Associate for the Program of Dialogue Between Science and Religion of the American Association for the Advancement of Science in Washington, D.C.

Susan L. Nelson is Associate Professor of Theology at Pittsburgh Theological Seminary in Pittsburgh, Pennsylvania.

Margaret Gray Towne teaches in the Department of Natural Science at Montana State University in Great Falls, Montana.